A. Johnson

Adverse Report of the Surveyor General of Arizona, Royal A. Johnson, upon the alleged Peralta Grant

A complete Expose of its fraudulent Character

A. Johnson

Adverse Report of the Surveyor General of Arizona, Royal A. Johnson, upon the alleged Peralta Grant

A complete Expose of its fraudulent Character

ISBN/EAN: 9783337070953

Printed in Europe, USA, Canada, Australia, Japan

Cover: Foto ©ninafisch / pixelio.de

More available books at **www.hansebooks.com**

ADVERSE REPORT OF

THE SURVEYOR GENERAL,

OF ARIZONA,

ROYAL A. JOHNSON,

UPON THE ALLEGED

PERALTA GRANT.

A Complete Expose of Its Fraudulent Character.

1890.

The Surveyor General's Report.

Under the power vested in me as Surveyor General of Arizona by the Act of Congress approved July 15, 1870 entitled "An Act Making Appropriations for Sundry Civil Expenses of the Government for the Year ending June 30th, 1871, and for Other Purposes," wherein it was provided, "That it shall be the duty of the Surveyor General of Arizona, under such instructions as may be given by the Secretary of the Interior, to ascertain and report upon the origin, nature, character and extent of the claims to lands in said Territory, under the laws, usuages and customs of Spain and Mexico, and for this purpose he shall have all the power conferred and shall perform all the duties enjoined upon the Surveyor General of New Mexico by the eighth section of an act entitled "An Act to Establish the Offices of Surveyor General of New Mexico, Kansas and Nebraska, to Grant Donations to Actual

Settlers, and for Other Purposes," approved July 22nd, 1854, and his report shall be laid before Congress for such action thereon as shall be deemed just and proper."

The act creating the office of Surveyor General, referred to, provides that the Surveyor General in pursuit of the investigation of claims, or alleged grants "may issue notices, summon witnesses, administer oaths, and do other necessary acts in the premises."

I herewith submit my report on a claim made to an alleged land grant of enormous proportions, located by claimants within the Territory of Arizona, and commonly known and designated as the "Peralta Grant."

In proceeding to report on this grant that, Congress may realize the importance of this claim, I will state that the so-called "Peralta Grant" is claimed to cover an area of land approximating fifty miles wide by one hundred and fifty miles long, and includes everything valuable within its extensive boundaries, particularly claiming the minerals. As claimed the Peralta grant covers a very large proportion of the counties of Maricopa, Pinal, Graham, Gila and Apache and takes in more than half of the White Mountain or San Carlos Indian reservation and the major portion of the Pima and Maricopa Indian reservation. The latter Indians are pre-eminently the agricultural Indians of the Territory, and have fertile farms on their reservations. It is also claimed that the city of Phoenix, one of the largest and most prosperous cities of Arizona, together with Florence, Tempe, Globe, Silver King, Pinal, Casa Grande, Solomonville and other towns of great future promise are located within the confines. In fact this grant in its vast entirety covers a section of country populous and full of promise. In addition mines of great wealth, many of which are constant bullion producers, are located on the claimed grant.

Since the purchase of this Territory from Mexico, the United States Government has been issuing its patents, and giving its titles to residents on the alleged grant, and this has been particularly the case in the fertile valleys of the Gila and Salt rivers, towards which locality the tide of immigration has naturally drifted and today the people on the alleged grant are resting secure in the possession of government titles to their homes, and other property.

As long as this land grant title hovers over the section of country claimed, without action, there must necessarily be retarded prosperity in that locality and it becomes the duty of those having cognizance of cases of this nature to act as expeditiously as possible.

In my report I shall maintain: First, That the King never recommended the grant as alleged by claimants. Second, That no such grant as the alleged Peralta Grant was ever made by the Viceroy of New Spain. Third, That admitting the legality of the alleged grant there are no legal claimants before this office, and none in existence so far as the records show. Fourth, That again admitting its legality, it is absolutely impossible to establish its boundaries, the alleged grant never having been bounded or surveyed, and without identified boundaries it fails.

The papers filed in this case by the several claimants are as follows: I will give the original petition of James Addison Reavis in full as it is an important factor in the consideration of the alleged grant. It was filed March 27th, 1883.

"To the Hon. J. W. Robbins.

United States Surveyor General for Arizona:

The petition of James Addison Reavis respectfully sets forth: That he is owner, by purchase from the legal heirs and representatives of the original grantee of a certain tract of land, situated in the Territory of Arizona, containing three hundred square leagues (Castilian or Spanish measurement) granted on the third day of January, 1758, by the Viceroy of New Spain to Don Miguel Peralta, Baron of the Coloradoes under royal decree of the King of Spain, directing such grant to be made to the said Peralta in consideration of and as a reward for distinguished military services rendered to the Crown in the war of Spain, as set forth in the following muniments of title:

First. "Royal decree signed at Madrid on the 20th of December 1748, directing grant to be made to Miguel de Peralta, Baron of the Coloradoes, of three hundred square leagues of land, or 19,200,000,000 square varas, Castilian or Spanish measurement, to be located on the royal lands in the northern portion of the Vice Royalty of New Spain.

Second. "Report of the Royal Inquisition in the city and arch bishopric of Mexico, dated October 1757, setting out that they make no opposition to the location as selected by Peralta. That as the concession will be attended with beneficial results, they have determined to recommend that the location be made so as to include the Gila river, to the north of the Mission of San Javier, the tract granted extending ten leagues from north to south and thirty leagues from east to west.

Third. Grant made by the Viceroy on the 3rd of January 1758, in accordance with royal decree, and the recommendation of the Royal Holy Tribunal of the Inquisition, giving to Peralta 300 square leagues, to be located according to the recommendation of the Royal Tribunal of the Inquisition, granting with the land all the minerals, waters and streams, together with all things thereto pertaining.

Fourth. Statement of Peralta, dated 13th of May 1758, showing by metes and bounds the location of the land granted

Fifth. Petition of Peralta to Carlos III, King of Spain, dated August 1st 1768, asking confirmation of a concession made to him (Peralta) by Ferdinand VI. and the location thereof by order of the Viceroy in 1758.

Sixth. Order of the King dated Madrid, January 20th, 1776, granting petition of Peralta.

All of which is fully and clearly set forth in original documents hereto annexed, marked "Exhibit A," with translation of same, which original documents are from the govern–

ment archives of the City of Mexico, and are made part of this petition.

Petitioner further represents that besides the original title papers procured from the government archives of the City of Mexico, a record of said grant is found in the proper office in the city of Guadalajara in Mexico, which city was at the date of the grant the place at which, under the then existing laws, grants of this character were required to be recorded, a transcript of which records, duly attested by the proper officers of the state of Jalisco, and officers of the Cabinet of the United States of Mexico and Secretary of Legation of the United States of America, is hereto annexed, marked "Exhibit B," with translation thereof, and made a part of this petition.

And your petitioner further states that a record of said grant, together with a copy of the last will and testament of the said Peralta, Baron of the Colorados, was made in the year 1788, in the ancient mission San Francisco Javier del Bac, giving to the legatee, Miguel Peralta, absolute possession and control of said grant, photographic copies of which, duly attested, are hereunto annexed, and marked "Exhibit C. 1-2-3 which, with translations of the same, are made part hereof.

Petitioner alleges that under and by virtue of the above described grant, Miguel de Peralta, Baron of the Colorados, became, in the year 1758, the owner in absolute property of the tract of land as described in the title papers above referred to, with all things thereunto pertaining, under the highest title that could be given to the royal domain in any part of the Spanish dominions, in the year 1758, towit: A grant by the King with title to nobility for distinguished military services to the crown, and that grants of such extent, or even greater, were, during the times of the Spanish rule in America, under similiar circumstances, often made is historically notorious.

Petitioner further alleges, that it being shown by the original title papers that in the year 1758, an absolute title becoming vested in Miguel de Peralta de la Cordoba, Baron of the Colorados, to the tract of land as hereinbefore described the right so possessed by him under the law was bequeathed to Miguel Peralta, his legal heir and representative. And petitioner represents that the present ownership of the tract of land granted in 1758 to Miguel de Peralta is clearly shown by the following chain of title.

First. Will of grantee dated in Guadalajara, January 13th, 1788 as set out in Exhibit B and C 1-2-3, hereinbefore referred to by which will Miguel de Peralta, Baron of the Colorados, left to his son Miguel Peralta, the tract of land described in said grant.

Second. Deed from Miguel Peralta to George M. Willing, dated October 20th, 1864.

Third. Power of attorney from George M. Willing to F. A. Massol, dated May 11th. 1864.

Fourth. Deed from Massol, attorney in fact of George M. Willing, to J. A. Reavis, dated May 22nd 1867.

Fifth. Deed from Florin A. Massol and wife to James Addison Reavis, dated July 29th, 1881.

Sixth. Deed from Mary Ann Willing, widow of George M. Willing, deceased, to James Addison Reavis, dated May 1st, 1882.

Petitioner alleges and claims that under and by virtue of the original title papers and the several powers of attorney and conveyances hereinbefore described, he is now the owner in the property or tract of land as granted, in the year 1758 by the Spanish government to Miguel de Peralta, Baron of the Colorados, as the same is described in the original title papers; and he therefore prays the Hon. Surveyor General of the United States of America that after the necessary examination he recommend a confirmation thereof to petitioner, and the issue of a patent to him by the government of the United States of America for the tract of land as described in the original title papers, in Castilian or Spanish measurement which equals 49¾ English miles in width north and south by 149¼ English miles in length east and west, be the same more or less.

JAMES ADDISON REAVIS,
Tucson, A. T., March 27th, 1883.

The other papers filed in addition to the petition of Reavis consist of:

The papers bound together in pamphlet form, with cotton cloth back and distinctly claimed by petitioner Reavis in his petition, dated March 27th, 1883, as "Original Title Papers". (This claim as to these papers being original title papers Reavis abandons in his late deraignment of title in his wife.) These bound papers consist of:

The royal decree (cedula) ordering grant.

The report of the Royal Inquisition.

The alleged grant by the Viceroy,

A statement in writing by Peralta showing the approximate location of the land.

A petition by Peralta to Carlos III. of Spain asking confirmation of grant.

An order of the King dated January 20th, 1776, at Madrid, Spain.

A letter from Santa Ana, President of the Mexican Republic, to Senor Don Miguel de Peralta, son of original grantee.

Three photographs of books of records of San Xavier church.

A copy of will of grantee dated in Guadalajara, January 13th, 1788, filed March 27th, 1883.

A deed from Miguel Peralta to George M. Willing dated October 20th, 1864.

A power of attorney from George M. Willing to F. A. Massol, dated May 11th, 1864.

A deed from Massol, attorney in fact of George M. Wiling to J. A. Reavis, dated May 22nd, 1867. (See Massol affidavits that deed is a forgery.)

A deed from Florin A. Massol and wife to James Addison Reavis, dated July 29th, 1881. (Of no import if valid as there is nothing to show that Massol ever had any right to the Peralta grant, even if found to be genuine.)

A deed from Mary Ann Willing, widow of George M. Willing, deceased, to James Addison Reavis, dated May 1st, 1882.

A sketch of the alleged grant and accompanying petition for survey.

Photographs of Maricopa mountains and "Monumental Rock", so named by Reavis) filed September 2nd, 1887.

Amended deraignment of title, filed September 2nd, 1887

Marriage contract and identity of heir at law, filed September 2nd, 1887.

Photographic copy of testimonia.

A bound book marked on outside cover as follows:

"Exhibits 'AAA' and 'BBB' Royal Patent, also Wills, Codicils and Certified Copy of Possession Given to Don Miguel de Peralta de la Cordoba, Baron of the Colorados, of Baronial Estate in Arizona," said to contain papers indicated by the markings on the cover.

In addition to the above a deed purporting to be from George M. Willing, (father of Dr. George M. Willing, deceased), to Brittain A. Hill is on file, and two reports made by Rufus C. Hopkins and a brief in the case by Hon. Clark Churchill, also a brief by Reavis. The above enumerated papers, together with some unimportant letters, complete the papers in the case. The alleged title papers filed originally in the office of the United States Surveyor-General (March 27th, 1883), upon which the claimant to the so-called Peralta Grant made his entire claim to the property as defined in the petition of Reavis, were bound together in pamphlet form by a cotton cloth back, and consist of a title page and six other pages of printed and written matter, all in the Spanish language. Nothing of a satisfactory nature was filed contemporaneously or has been since to show how claimant Reavis, who filed these papers, got possession of what he termed "Original Papers" at the time of filing. Nothing as to where these "Original Papers" had been for the one hundred and thirty years or more during which period of time they are claimed to have been in existence. Nothing even as to who the last man was that transferred these old papers to Reavis or whence they came in any instance. They are simply produced by Reavis, and this office is given to understand that the papers are simon pure productions from the proper sources. The claimant Reavis did make an oral statement of a romantic nature to me personally to the effect that long after Dr. Willing's death in Yavapai county, through whom Reavis originally claimed title, he (Reavis), went to Yavapai county in search of any effects belonging to the deceased Dr. Willing and finally his trip was made fruitful by finding the papers above referred to stored away in an old cabin attic in a gunny or grip sack, from which place of deposit he managed dexterously to take them without the knowledge of the then custodian, an ex-probate official of Yavapai county, Arizona, so that claimant cannot even prove that he got the papers in the way claimed, or that they were ever even in Dr. Willing's possession; but I want to call particular attention right here to the fact that claimant Reavis alleged that the papers were in Dr. Willing's possession in view of the fact of his having abandoned this deraignment of title through the said Dr. Willing, alleging that such deraignment was void; that Dr. Willing never had a bona fide title; in other words that Peralta deeding to Willing had no title whatever; in fact was a fraud. How, then, in light of claimant's own assertions regarding the title, did Dr. Willing become possessed of what claimant asserted to be original title papers, and where did he get them if the Peralta who deeded the property to him had no title to it, but was a fraud, and how did Reavis find them among

Willing's papers? Thus Reavis fails to account in the very first instance how he came to possess the papers originally depended on to prove his title, or if we accept his romantic story of their recovery from Dr. Willing's effects he places them in the hands of a man whom he now alleges had no title, and makes him the last custodian before the petitioner Reavis. It may be that the object of the letter on the last sheet of the document under consideration, said to be from Santa Ana, President of the Mexican Republic, is to account for the presence in this country of these papers, making it appear that Santa Ana, President of a Republic, sent them to the man Peralta, who deeded to Willing at Wickenburg, from whom Willing possibly received them at the same time he is said to have received the deed. If the claimant takes this stand then he has to maintain according to the title he now alleges as the perfect one, that Santa Ana, President of the Republic of Mexico, took the trouble to gather up original papers from the archives of Mexico and send them to a stranger in the United States without the stranger being satisfactorily identified, and as a result of such gross carelessness on President Santa Ana's part, he sent them to a fraud in the person of the man Peralta, from whom Willing is supposed to have received the deed for the property. This must be Reavis' position, and all this is highly improbable and does not bear the impress of truth or ordinary sense or reflect credit on the claimant. Governments, and particularly the Spanish and Mexican people, zealously look after their archives and pride themselves on their system of records, and they do not at the mere solicitation of an absolute stranger deplete their archves by gathering up and sending original papers of great value to unknown persons. At the time Reavis filed Santa Ana's alleged letter to account for the papers being in the hands of the Miguel Peralta of Wickenburg, and through him in Dr. Willing's possession, he was claiming under a deraignment of title through Dr. Willing and the Wickenburg Peralta. In proceeding to consider the documents originally filed by Reavis, and alleged to have been found by Reavis at Prescott among Dr. Willing's long neglected posthumos effects, upon which Reavis originally rested his whole title, I shall take the ground that he filed for consideration all the papers he could possibly produce at that time, and that he rested his case and he certainly closed his exparte showing by submitting his brief. The other claimants likewise produced in those same papers the best results obtainable. I shall consider these papers in the light of their competentcy as evidence in support of the claim set up.

The first or title sheet is old and dilapidated, full of holes where the ink is supposed to have eaten through or where the paper is supposed to have yielded to the ravages of time. In its upper left hand corner, over what may be sealing wax, is what appears to be a small, irregular piece of bond or parchment paper, pasted on without any apparent significance or meaning. The front of the sheet is printed Spanish and reads as follows:

"Book which only serves to note therein the deposits that may be delivered to me by order of the Royal Holy Inquisition for the proofs of petitioners that may be as a depos.tory of the same, June 23rd, 1768."

Now this frontispiece to this remarkable production of alleged antiquity would indicate that it was a cover to a book of records of the acts of the Inquisition, and certainly leads me to suspect that it was copied from some such book. In this particular instance it seems much out of place, as what follows this original sheet under consideration is not such records as are kept by such officials as the reading on the page would indicate, the reading on the page would make the man in whose possession it is, a recorder of papers of the Holy Inquisition, and should appear on the cover of a general record book of such papers; instead of which it is filed here as a frontispiece of half a dozen pages of matter, all of which pages appertain to the alleged grant of Peralta, and in no way, shape or form, go to make up several acts of the Royal Inquisition, as the page referred to indicates.

This page simply plays no important part whatever in this case, and is not germane to its consideration, but I want to call particular attention to the fact that the name Peralta does not even appear in any way, shape or form on this outside sheet, as would naturally be expected. On the back of this front or title page, on which it will be remembered is pasted a yellow sheet of thin parchment paper, calculated to hide from view the back of the title page. By raising this yellow sheet of paper it was found that the great defect of the title sheet had been remedied by the following words in writing: 'In relation to the concession to the Senor Don Miguel de Peralta, Baron of the Colorados."

This writing has been added to the back of this page within a few years, and of course was placed there for the purpose of connecting the title sheet with Don Miguel de Peralta. It is written with a steel pen, hair lines being apparent throughout the entire writing, and the ink used seems to be the same as that in which the King's name is signed on the succeeding pages.

The person adding this writing evidently appreciated the importance of connecting the outside page with Don Miguel de Peralta. The next page is mostly printed in beautiful type. I have examined this printing very critically in connection with printing done in Mexico during the same century by the Inquisition. I find an altogether different appearance in the printing under discussion from those papers issued by the Inquisition from the City of Mexico, with which I have compared it. (See letter herewith from Assistant Librarian of Congress, to whom I submitted a photographic copy of this printing for comparison). One very important difference is that while the papers filed by Reavis invariably shows a fine cut shapely modern S, whether the letters appear in the middle or at the end of the word; the documents issued by the Inquisition used both the old-fashioned and modern S according to their position in the word, and the modern S is not the shapely S used in the Peralta papers; some writing and rubricas appear on this sheet. "Yo el Rey" is printed at the bottom of the printed matter. A seal printed on the paper also appears. It is not impressed on the paper, and has no special significance unless to simply indicate that it was used on a great deal of paper of this kind, therefore by proper inference if used in large quantities for like purposes it would be comparatively easy to obtain and would not be difficult to duplicate. The signature of the Senor Minister of State, "Don Jose de Carvajal y Lancaster," is printed, and under it appears a rubrica. There are many rubricas over this sheet and the claimants fail to offer any evidence whatever as to whose rubricas they are. It is not to be supposed that a grant fifty by one hundred and fifty miles of the best land in Arizona is to pass on the strength of a few rubricas that any boy might imitate without corroborative evidence as to the genuineness. It is my experience that even genuine rubricas vary very much. In considering a document of the import of the one at present under consideration, we would naturally suppose that it would be taken from department to department of the government, to receive the several signatures and rubricas this page purports to convey and that considerable variation would appear in the pens and ink used; but an appearance of similiarity is uniformly preserved throughout the entire page. To the right of the small seal printed on the paper above referred to, the Senior Minister of the Council of State certifies that he has annexed the great seal of the state to the sheet. This expression of the Minister of State would lead us to expect that the impress of the great seal of state would be found impressed or attached to the sheet. Nothing of the kind appears, and in place of the attached seal that the Minister seems to refer to, we simply have a little printed seal. This little printed seal may have been printed on reams of blank paper used for royal purposes during the past century; if such was the case it would not be difficult to secure a sheet of paper with this small seal printed thereon and add above such seal the printed matter which is found above the seal under consideration and which presents such a modern appearance as far as the type used is concerned. It will be borne in mind that the claimant Reavis under the present claim of his wife does not assert this sheet to be the original "Cedula of Ferdinand the VI," but produces in his new claim what he asserts to be the original "Cedula."

Under these circumstances I would like to ask claimant *how all the prior alleged original rubricas came on this sheet if it is not an original cedula as formerly claimed by Reavis?*

This remarkable sheet is dated January 3rd, 1748. A paper of this description counts for nothing in considering the case, as its validity is in no way proven. Nothing to show that it is an original document or a bona fide reproduction of the same is offered. It is simply submitted for what it is worth, and is not competent evidence in the consideration of a case either in court or in the office of a Surveyor-General. Much of the writing on this sheet bears evidence of having been done with a steel pen, which, of course, is impossible if the document was executed at the date it is alleged to have been, as the steel pen made its first appearance in an imperfect condition in 1803, but was not made useful for many years after that date. On this sheet also appears "Yo el Rey" with a rubrica, represented of course to be the King's, and judging from the date in connection therewith, December 2d, 1772, it is meant for the rubrica of Carlos III of Spain. The American Minister at Madrid in answer to a letter from me, sent through the Interior and State Departments during my previous term as Surveyor-General, sent me a tracing of the name of Carlos III, signed by the King in 1759, and it appears as "Carlos" with a rubrica. This plays no important part, as it was customary to sign documents "Yo el Rey." The "Yo el Rey" appears to have been written with a stub pen or quill. Nothing appears on this page entitled to credit, considered without corroborating evidence. This document was primarily alleged to be the original cedula or decree of King Ferdinand the VI, ordering the grant to be made, and was presented to this office as such, though now one of the claimants, Reavis, claims to have since discovered the original cedula in Spain, and now if he attaches any importance whatever to the paper he originally urged upon this office as the original cedula, which I am now considering, it must be a mere copy.

This is an important feature in the case, showing how completely claimant Reavis has abandoned what he originally presented as his title papers, without submitting any good reason for doing so. A good reason, however, may be supplied claimant Reavis when the Massol affidavit is taken into consideration. Next in order considering this document comes three pages of written matter in the same handwriting. It purports to be a copy of the report of the Inquisition on the grant proposed to be given to Peralta and also a copy of the grant as actually made by the Viceroy of New Spain, as well as a lame descript tion of the locus of the grant. The original report of the Inquisition and the original grant of the Viceroy made about the middle of the last century are not produced, and unquestionably have not been found; but in lieu of the original papers so very important in considering this case these poor substitutes are produced. Why the locus of the original cannot be established when correct copies can be made from them I am at a loss to understand. Reason dictates that if bona fide copies from originals on file can be produced there ought to be no trouble in locating the place of deposit of such originals.

When we stop and reflect on the learned body of men comprising the Holy Inquisition this alleged copy is but a sorry exhibit of their handiwork at producing certified records. It lacks every appearance, (with the possible exception of old age) that would naturally be expected in a certified record of such important documents by such an educated body of men.

This paper demands our careful attention, as it is a paper playing no unimportant part in considering the question whether these papers have not been fabricated in aid of establishing a title to a large proportion of our territory. At the end of the pages under consideration appear the words "A Copy, June 23rd, 1768," and a large seal, claimed to be the seal of the Inquisition. This seal is not impressed on the page proper, but is on a separate piece of parchment paper pasted on the page. When claimant Reavis filed his "original" papers he pointed to the seal of the Inquisition as being conclusive evidence of the genuineness of the paper bearing its impress. Being desirous of ascertaining how difficult it would be to procure these seals of the Inquisition and to satisfy myself as to the probability of a person being able to secure them for the purpose of fabricating a paper purporting to be from the Holy Inquisition of New Spain, I sent a letter to the proper Mexican authorities, and as a result a duplicate of the seal produced on the Peralta papers has been furnished me. The following is a quotation from the letter sending the seals: "I enclose three documents found in said archives and which could be spared from them, containing the impress of the seal of the said ecclesiastical tribunal." The attachment of the seal of the Holy Inquisition to the paper filed by Reavis carries no weight whatever with me under the circumstances, inasmuch as I have been able to secure from Mexico an exact duplicate which I could attach to as solemn a document as Reavis claims his document to be in the space of one minute. The production of the counterpart of his seal, so easily obtained and the wording of letter transmitting them, shows beyond controversy that the impress was readily obtainable and thereafter could be utilized for the fabrication of papers.

One very noticeable feature in comparing the seal of the Inquisition obtained by me from undoubted sources of validity with that filed in the case by Reavis on his document, is that the seal obtained by me was impressed on the paper with a metal seal, which, while it made its impress on the face of the seal, at the same time made a corresponding impress on the back of the parchment paper to which said seal was attached, while the seal on the Reavis documents appears to be simply pasted on the paper under consideration and shows no evidence whatever of having been impressed thereon by a metal seal; the parchment paper directly back of such seal of the Inquisition is smooth, its smoothness evidently being foreign to any impress whatever. Although the seal obtained by me is much older than the period in which the Reavis seal is alleged to have been attached, it does not present the brown appearance of the Reavis seal. Said brown color looking as though it might have been scorched by being heated over a flame for detachment from its original resting place, or in placing it in its present position. In further proof it is cracked as though scorched. It is folly to talk about land grant records from the archives of the Inquisition as the law existed.

At this stage of this report it must be borne in mind that the all important paper of this claim, the paper whose existence must be proven or the claim that such a grant ever existed for a moment must fall to the ground, is the *original grant of the Viceroy*. This paper must be produced to show that the *words of recommendation* attributed to Ferdinand VI in his communication to the Viceroy had received any weight in the eyes of the Viceroy, or that he had acted on the King's suggestion and made a grant to Peralta. Of course if claimants cannot in a perfectly clear way prove that the Viceroy granted the land their case is at an end. The King's words, if we allow that he wrote them, or caused them to be written, were only words of recommendation, and it was left to the Viceroy to carry out the granting of the land if he saw fit and to refuse to do so if he saw fit.

It now becomes an all important proposition in the support of this claim to get the original "grant" of the Viceroy or it that cannot be done in a manner satisfactory to the government for the plaintiffs to secure such a copy of the original as the claimants consider the government will recognize. To this end are produced the papers under consideration. No certificate of a modern date nor any other reliable certification appears on the copies which would point to [the originals being at present in the custody of some custodian of archives where they could be readily located and seen, but the certification of the copies is remarkably ancient and unsatisfactory, and nothing is at hand of an acceptable nature in a court or in this office to enable me to ascertain the whereabouts of originals or to prove their existence, and if they were to be obtained it is the duty of the claimants to produce them or to obtain and submit undoubted proof of their existence in their proper archives.

The above referred to certified copy is produced without showing where it was certified from, unless the writing is under the seal of the Inquisition, and it is expected by the claimants that this poor specimen of a copy shall play an important part in the question of the validity of the grant. The inability to ascertain where this paper was written or the place of deposit of the originals invalidates the entire paper. The signature and rubricas attached to this document have the appearance of being written by one man, with the same pen and ink, and could be easily reproduced by a good penman. The paper looks old. I want to particularly impress upon the mind the fact that the copy of, or possibly, it may be claimed, the original of the Viceroy's grant is claimed to have been on deposit in the archives of the Holy Inquisition, whence the copies under consideration are al'eged to have come certified by the priests, otherwise, of course, the alleged copies could not have been made from the ecclesiastical archives.

By what propriety an original grant, or a copy of such a grant, by a Viceroy should leave its natural channel in the governmental archives to become part and parcel of the ecclesiastical records is not shown. It is certainly out of place among such records.

The last sheet of this document is covered with writing, rubricas, etc. On one side is what purports to be a letter from Miguel Peralta to the King of Spain, Carlos III asking a reconfirmation of the grant, and his (Peralta's) location of the same. He particularly states that his land contain- much mineral. It is dated in Mexico, the first of August 1768, when Peralta, according to claim, was an old man. The writing is made to appear as the writing of an aged and decrepit man, Below this letter something is written which it is impossible to correctly decipher on account of its torn and mutilated condition, but it is evidently intended for some writing in connection with the King's alleged signature on the following page, in confirming the grant to Peralta, as at the top of the other side of the sheet, the last page of the papers bound together, appears "January 22nd 1776," "Yo el Rey," with rubrica, without the slightest mention of Peralta or his alleged grant or any words of confirmation. The signature "Yo el Rey" and the rubrica following, in both instances, are unquestionably written by the same person, and are claimed to have been attached by Carlos III, when the papers were returned to him for reconfirmation by Miguel Peralta. A difference of over three years is made to appear in the dates connected with these signatures. The first signature has preceding it "Passed before me, dated in Madrid on the second of December 1772, Yo el Rey." The last signature is claimed to be the King's and alleged to have been attached at the same time when Peralta asked for reconfirmation has the date "January 22nd, 1776." How this occurred, or how it is to be accounted for no evidence is offered to show, but under the circumstance it is a very noticeable discrepancy. Following "Yo el Rey" and the rubrica referred to is a seal similar to the one described by me as being on the title of first page. It looks like a daub of sealing wax, with a little piece of parchment paper stuck on while hot, and is about the size of a five cent nickel piece.

Nothing is filed to show how this last paper became attached to the other papers unless some writing at the foot of the page, badly torn and disfigured with parts of the paper missing, is allowed to account for it. It is filed as a letter from Santa Ana, President of the Mexican Republic, to Miguel de Peralta, son of the original grantee, then living at San Diego, California.

He goes on to say to the son of the grantee, that diligent search has been made, through his several ministers, for the papers relating to the concession to his father, and that *all that could be found* he sent to him, and in relation to the portion lying in the United States of Mexico he assures the son he will be secure with these papers, although he has separated the originals; and he believes he will be equally secure in that part lying in the United States. The letter is dated May 10th, 1853.

Now this would seem to intimate that Santa Ana had possibly fastened these papers together in sending them to Peralta's son; but this would be contradictory of the idea that Peralta himself had submitted all these papers together to Carlos III, with his letter asking reconfirmation, four score years *before*, and the claim that King Carlos III, had signed the document twice, once on the first, (or Ferdinand's cedula sheet) and once on the last page, would go to show that the papers were together when submitted to him, provided his signatures are genuine; instead of having been gathered together by Santa Ana in 1853. Then again the two small seals claimed to be royal seals, appear on the front or title page and on the back page after the alleged signature of Carlos III, seeming to be exact duplicates.

An inconsistency at least is apparent as to when these papers were first gotten together. The whole document to my mind, where writing or printing appears, shows the probability of being a modern production. It is not to be entertained as evidence as it appears of record in this office, and must remain a lot of unauthenticated copies at best, and can in no way be considered as competent evidence to the validity of the Peralta claim as it in no way establishes the grant by the Viceroy.

If I admit, for the sake of argument, that the alleged letter of Santa Ana is genuine, he practically informs young Peralta of the loss of the originals, and that his claim in the United States without them is doubtful, and further informs him that they have sent all the documents that a very careful search brought to light.

The letter of Santa Ana's, if genuine, would only be important to show, that though the records of Mexico were searched with all the great facilities of the government itself at the instigation of the President of that Government no other papers were on file anywhere, consequently a natural deduction is that papers now found were surreptiously put in the archives after President Santa Ana's thorough search *had failed to find them.*

The claimants in urging the validity of Santa Ana's letter really put a quietus on their production of any more papers from the Mexican archives. Still the claimant Reavis produces, as will be seen hereafter, further papers from Guaalajara, the very first place where President Santa Ana would naturally look for official documents, that being one of the proper places of record of such documents as belonged to New Spain; and Reavis although a private citizen of a foreign country accomplishes what President Santa Ana, with all his great power, could not accomplish.

I will say in closing my examination of the papers originally filed that where writing appears for the royal signature to follow it is of a character that might be attributed to a twelve-year old schoolboy, instead of bearing out the reputation possessed by Spain at that time of being in advance of the world's civilization in this respect. The whole appearance of the papers is against their validity. These papers were filed by Reavis as the evidence of his claim to be one of the largest land owners in the world, and at the same time of their filing, and for a long time thereafter, he, as well as the other claimants, rested their entire case on their merits, claiming that even if they could not prove the first printed page ordering the Viceroy to make the grant to be an originrl cedula of the King Ferdinand VI, it was finally made an original by the reconfirmation of Carlos III, when he twice attached his royal signature to the papers, and it is my opinion that the whole object of the signature of Carlos III was to fill the void created by inability to plausibly produce the original recommendation of the King, Ferdinand VI, or the original grant by the Viceroy of New Spain. The claim however that the signature of Carlos III made the paper an original grant is farcical. By their own showing the claimants make Peralta the sender of the papers to the King, and it is represented that Carlos III, upon the mere statement by Peralta that he had such a grant, confirmed the grant that the Viceroy had made. It seems to me that the allegation that Peralta ever sent the papers to Carlos III with the representation that he had a grant, and asked him to confirm it, is a shrewd move, to formulate a new and equally fraudulent claim in case the Viceroy claim failed on account of close research. Why, I want to ask, if Peralta had received a grant of land from the Viceroy under the recommendation of King Ferdinand VI, which claimants assert positively carried minerals, etc., in specific terms in the original grant by the Viceroy, did Peralta take the trouble to have it all done over again by Carlos III when Peralta should have been in full possession more than ten years before? I cannot entertain such a silly proposition, and I think it only figures in this case to help the claim out on account of the original grant itself being absent and unaccounted for. Then if Peralta, the grantee, had the original papers, especially the grant by the Viceroy, why did he not send them to Carlos III? The King, Carlos III, don't say he makes a grant; he is made to appear in the light of attaching his signature to a grant already made, and the way his name appears on the last sheet withou the words of confirmation on the same sheet even or legible, makes the whole proposition absurd.

I want to call attention here to the fact that although the

King in his alleged order to the Viceroy to make the grant explicitly states that it is upon the recommendation of the Inquisition still the claimants do not file or allege that they have found the original recommendation of the Inquisition prior to 1748 (when Ferdinand VI is said to have made the grant) and inasmuch as they have produced similiar evidence from the records of the Inquisition, I am wholly unable to understand how so important a document as this original recommendation was not found, if in existence, as on account or its being the original act of the Inquisition that brought about the alleged action of Ferdinand VI, it should by all means have been produced from the archives. I don't want to confound the original recommendation of the Inquisition prior to the year 1748, *which I now ask for*, and which the king refers to in his alleged recommendation to the viceroy, with the alleged copy that is produced of an alleged report of the Inquisition in the premises. This latter act of the Inquisition purporting to be the report on the location, etc., occurred several years after King Ferdinand's alleged recommendation to the viceroy.

Ferdinand VI is also made to refer in his recommendation to the viceroy to a recommendation to him of a "consulado" and "superior judge" approved by the government and presented to the general military board. Claimants do not account for the non production of the originals or satisfactory copies of these papers, and say nothing as to where they are. They ought to be easily produced.

One of the most important facts to consider in this paper, the sheets of which are pasted together with cloth, is that neither on the title page (where it properly belongs) nor on the last page where the king's signature is alleged to be signed does the name of Miguel Peralta appear or anything in connection with a grant to him; which founds a very reasonable suspicion that these pages might have been used originally for some other purpose. In connection with the king's alleged approval of the grant, nothing but the date above the alleged signature of the king appears on this page. This creates a very strong suspicion of fraud. The writing stating the object of the king's signature *is on the preceding page*. To me this is very conclusive evidence that these outside sheets may at some past time have been used for other purposes, for certainly the outside sheets of so important a document should have noted the name of the grantee and his title, etc. Nothing of the kind appears, but on the contrary they might be today attached to *other interior contents*, with the same degree of propriety that they at present nestle under their protecting sheets, such suspicious looking documents as those relied on by the claimants to the Peralta grant. This ommission of Peralta's name in the title on these outside pages is no ordinary omission; it is a most extraordinary defect. In addition the ragged and unintelligible writing at the bottom of the last page, claimed to be from Santa Ana, adds nothing to the genuineness of this suspicious page. In its mutilated condition it can receive no serious attention and presents no evidence of being genuine. It may be asserted that the alleged king's signature (Carlos III) on the page containg the alleged order of the King Ferdinand VI strengthens the genuine appearance of the document. To this I would answer that the king's signature on the last page, admitting it to be genuine, for the sake of argument, but to have been originally used for some other purpose, which the sheets would seem to indicate was the case, on account of the absence above the king's signature of anything appertaining to Peralta, would furnish the very means to aid its being successfully duplicated on the page containing Ferdinand's cedula.

A paper is presented to this office from Guadalajara as a certified copy of papers on file at Guadalajara, found there by Reavis in the face of the assurance by President Santa Ana, in his alleged letter (filed by claimant Reavis) that with all the facilities as prsideent of the republic he could not find any such papers in any archives of the republic, and Guadalajara it is to be presumed is the place where Santa Ana would have given careful search. The records at Guadalajar have been loosely kept, only a small portion of them being bound;

the balance have been kept for a long period of time in boxes, easy of access, and easily added to by a person taking the necessary time to accomplish such an object. Binding of the records was going on in 1883 and for some time before, and as a consequence records that were loosely scattered in 1881–1882 or 1883 might be found in a bound condition a year or so later. The Mexican archives were so loosely protected in Guadalajara as to create suspicion where papers are found by a foreigner that the president of the republic himself and his machinery of the state sought in vain to find. Mr. R. C. Hopkins, then an employee of the Surveyor Generals office, in his report about the Guadalajara papers says:

"The archives in Guadalajara formerly consisted of unbound papers, with the exception of a few books *bound in parchment*, after the old style and, like the archives of all Spanish countries, consisted of official correspondence and decrees, civil and criminal proceedings, and in fact of all such official papers as would naturally be produced by the machinery of such governments as those of Spain and Mexico. The greater portion of these miscellaneous archives have within the last few years been bound for preservation by the state department as appropriations have been from time to time made for that purpose, and in one of these volumes, *thus bound within the past two years*, are found the papers in relation to the Peralta grant. These title papers show folding marks, as do many others in the books referred to. Most of the records of archives from the years 1740 to 1760 appear to have been destroyed, as I was informed by the archivero."

Now we have this statement of Santa Ana that the papers could not be found, and we have also the information that most of the records between 1740 and 1760 were destroyed, but Reavis produces from a newly bound volume that, according to Mr. Hopkins, was bound in 1881, the copies of the papers he sought.

Mr. Hopkins says in his report: "It is important to ascertain, if possible, if these title papers be historically consistent, that is, if the parties whose names appear therein did

in fact exist, and if they occupied the positions as stated in the papers at the respective dates mentioned *   *   *
*   *   *   Contemporaneous history, found in Bancroft's library in the city of San Francisco, California, shows that the above named individuals (referring to names on the papers) were living and acting in the capacities above stated at the date mentioned in the report. except it appears that Father Tameron, is mentioned by the historian as bishop of Durango, New Mexico, at the time, belongs to the bishopric Durango."

This kind of an investigation amounts to next to nothing, as what was accessible to a man examining into the matter would likewise be accessible to a person desirous of making up a perfect record to formulate grant papers. In fact to secure names of officials contemporaneous with the grant would be the first step in a chain of fraud.

Mr. Hopkins says: "The *original grant by the viceroy not being produced*—his signature is not found among the title papers. In 1758 the Marquis de las Amarillas filled the office of viceroy of New Spain,"

Mr. Hopkins further says in his report: "One of the papers found in the government archives at Guadalajara is 'Testimonio Original' This paper is a copy of the decree of Ferdinand VI recommending the grant. This testimonio (certified copy) is authenticated by these signatures made with rubricas alone."

Mr. Hopkins goes on to say that rubricas similar to those referred to above are found on other papers issued contemperaneous with the decree of Ferdinand VI. The papers filed in this office from Guadalajara amount to this: A petition by Reavis dated November 27th, 1883, to the Second General Court, wherein he represents himself as the rightful owner of the "Peralta Hacienda" in Arizona, that he had in his possession a copy, and a photograph of a document, and a map of said property, which, with the consent of the governor of that state, was issued to him in 1881, (the very year that Hopkins says the book containing the records was being bound) by the person in charge of the archives at Guadalajara, which show a concession made to Don Miguel Peralta. Petitioner then prays that the court will issue the necessary order to the public register in charge of the records, etc., directing him to issue to the petitioner a "testimonio" of the record. The above petition shows that *Reavis was in communication with the Archivero at Guadalajara in* 1881 *when the important act of binding the volume within which was found the Peralta papers was being accomplished.*

The papers produced on this petition is a certified copy (which petitioner asserts he got from the proper officer) of copies of the alleged originals of Ferdinand's decree; the viceroy's grant; an uncertain description of the locus of the grant; a will of Peralta leaving grant to his son, and directing him to go and take possession. This certified copy of the copies of the several papers cited immediately above, which said copies are on file in Guadalajara, is presented to this office as evidence, and I am asked to give credit to a paper of this character found in a volume which had only been bound two years before produced; all of which copies were probably filed at one time, and by one man. Nothing is offered among the papers to show where the original papers were filed, and it is very remarkable that the original Peralta himself should not have given definite information about the originals, considering the great anxiety evidenced in his alleged will to have his son inherit his large donation of land.

These copies of copies would not make competent evidence in any court and are not admissable for serious consideration in this case. The production of copies taken from copies has proven the remarkable feature in this case. Copies from originals apparently being out of the question.

I will premise my consideration of the next paper filed in this case, by stating that on February 1st, 1884, I wrote a request to the Hon. Minister Plenipotentiary at Madrid asking him for certified copies of each and every important paper appertaining in any way to the alleged Peralta grant; and thinking that a request transmitted through the high medium of the state department might receive better attention on the part of the Spanish government, than one from this office direct, I sent an additional request to the Secretary of the Interior, which was transmitted through the state department with photographs etc. furnished by me, to secure a full and intelligent examination of the records of Madrid and Seville. I also took similiar steps to have the records of Mexico carefully searched. In response to these requests on May 2nd, 1885 I received a letter from the Commissioner of the General Land Office containing the following: "You are further advised that this department has received from the department of state official information communicated by the Spanish government, through the American legation at Madrid, that a careful search has been made by the Director of the Archives and that the so called Peralta grant does not exist in those archives."

The same letter says: "Thorough search has been made under the direction of the government of the Republic of Mexico at the instance of this government and no record of this grant nor any of the various minute proceedings required by the laws of Spain and the Indies connected with the making of such grants has been discovered."

Now here we have the highest possible authority from the proper sources, that nothing whatever could be found in the archives where such papers would naturally be kept, either in Spain or Mexico. These communications coming to the attention of the claimant Reavis, it is alleged he went to Spain and again succeeded, as he claims, in finding papers of alleged value to this claim in the archives there, and when he next appeared in the office of the Surveyor General he filed these papers with an amended deraignment of title, claiming the title for his wife as "SOFIA LORETA MICAELA MASO REAVIS PERALTA DE LA CORDOBA" and signs himself James Addison *Peralta* Reavis. All this on the strength of the papers found by Reavis in Spain, after the positive assurance by the Spanish government to our government that no such papers could be found. It is impossible for us to set aside the statement of a government and accept that of Reavis. In this last and most remarkable move everything appertaining to the original deraignment of title is apparently set aside by the new claimant, the wife of Reavis, without Reavis interfering in behalf of his orignal claim or offering anything in explanation of the abandonment of the former, and the adoption of the last filed claim. The latter claim is made in a matter of fact way, wholly ignoring Reavis (except as the husband of the claimant) and his former stupendous efforts to deraign title direct from the old Baron to himself. The claim as now made by the petitioners Reavis and wife, that the wife, the said "Sofia Loreta Micaela Maso Reavis de la Cordoba" is a lineal decendant, and sole heir to the original grantee of the alleged so called "Peralta Grant," being the great-grand-daughter of the original Peralta, and that she is entitled to the alleged grant as stated above. This petition was filed in the Surveyor General's office on the 2nd day of September, 1887. They also file a petition for a preliminary survey of the grant, and a map of the land they claim, and by them it is located about eight miles south of the former claim made by claimant when he was simply James Addison Reavis. Contemporaneous with the filing of the new claim to this colossal property, petitioners file photographic copies of Spanish documents, will, codicils, etc., which photographic copies are certified as true copies by the Secretary of the Interior under section 882 of the Revised Statutes providing that "Copies of any books, records, papers or documents in any of the executive departments, authenticated, under the seals of such department, respectively shall be admitted in evidence equally with the originals thereof." This section, by the words "originals thereof," evidently means the papers on file in the department from which the copies certified to as the copies by the department head, have been made; not necessarily the original title papers themselves, for the very papers filed in the department may be, and very probably are, only copies brought to the department and filed; from which, after they are filed, other copies may be made and certified to by the secretary of the department as correct copies of the papers on file in the department, be they copies or originals. To give any other meaning would make the department responsible as guaranteeing that copies of papers filed in the department were correct copies of bona fide orignals, or the originals themselves, and that surely was never intended

To give weight to copies produced here authenticated as provided for in the section referred to, I take it for granted that the Statute contemplated such documents as are properly on file in the department. The section certainly cannot mean that any paper may be placed in the files of a department, however wrongfully and merely upon the certification that a copy given to some one is a correct copy of the paper on file in the department, make that copy, so certified, competent evidence. Secretary Muldrow, in certifying to the copy produced in the Surveyor General's office certifies in the following language: "Pursuant to section 882 of the Revised Statutes' I hereby certify that the annexed is a true copy of a document on file in this department, except to the following discrepancies." (Noting them.) In no way does this certification bear out the idea that Secretary Muldrow meant to convey the fact that the papers were originals, or of any import as bona fide copies of originals. He simply says that they are copies of certain papers placed on file in the department adding nothing whatever of their history, and still these papers are brought before me and I am asked to give them weight in the matter under consideration. A more veritable farce in the annals of legal investigation was never enacted.

This office was the proper place of deposit for any papers the claimants wished considered in connection with this grant or attached any importance to. The other papers were filed here for the careful scrutiny of the Surveyor General. Why was such a marked departure observed in this last matter?

The papers filed, certified as shown above, consist of six photographs made in Washington. Nothing appears to show that any originals were produced to take the photographs from. No evidence is produced here to show where the originals are, or how he secured the copies. We can hardly be asked to believe that a foreign private citizen could secure papers that our government, with all the aid of the government machinery of Spain, found no trace of. It is asking too much of me to give credit to such a statement.

The photographs are alleged to represent the original cedula of Ferdinand VI, or royal patent. A will of the original grantee. Another will of the younger Peralta, the son of the original grantee, who in his will, lays the ground work for the change in the deraignment of title that has occurred, carefully reciting alleged facts that will be considered in connection with that part of the report that treats of the heirs, etc. The last Peralta also recites his muniments of title very minutely and speaks of the papers he refers to in his will in regard to title as "authenticated copies,"

During my previous term as surveyor general it was often remarked to Reavis that under even the most favorable circumstances, for instance, the production of the viceroy's grant, his grant would fail, as it was never taken possession of. What I consider as one of the most marvelous features of the last filings in the following quotation, alleged to have been recited in the last will of Peralta, the son of the grantee, but on no occasion by the grantee himself, viz: "We have given possession, in the name of his majesty the King, by command of the viceroy of New Spain. Done at the eastern base of the aforesaid Maricopa mountain, *and the drawing made on the rock, on this* 13*th day of May, in the year one thousand seven hundred and fifty-eight.*"

By the above we are given to understand that Don Miguel de Peralta, son of the alleged grantee, recites in his will in minute detail copies of papers to show the giving of possession to the property alleged to have been granted to his alleged father, and the identifying of the boundaries by a map on the rock. (The describing of the map on the rock, I am confident, was to change the boundaries and thus avoid the vigorous fighting of the Arizona Canal Company.) The claimants fail entirely to prove any connection whatever between the Peralta making the will in which the above passage about the map and possession being given appears, and the original grantee; even allowing such a grant was ever made to an original Peralta; or any connection with the Peralta at Wickenberg, Arizona. They do not show where the elder Peralta died, what children were left, or why we should take it for granted that the latter Peralta who so considerately recited so much in his will to favor the present claim of claimants, should in any way be considered as the son of Peralta and particularly as his only favored son.

By their two sets of claims they first prove that the son of Peralta, in Arizona, on October 20th, 1864, made a deed to Willing, and then claimant Reavis turns around and proves, with about the same show of probability and equal certainty, that before deeding to Willing he or *some other Peralta also claiming to be the son and sole heir*, attempted to make other disposition of the property on the 2nd day of January, 1863, by a will. By this new state of affairs Reavis' wife would cut out he St. Louis heirs claiming under the deed to Dr. Willing, and at the same time Reavis renders null and void all titles he issues while claiming under the same deed from Peralta, the alleged son, to Dr. Willing, for which deeds Reavis is said to have received large sums of money.

Nothing is offered by claimants to harmonize these discrepancies about the Peraltas, the wills, deeds, codicils, etc. I am simply left to solve the proposition. In showing the fact that the grant would fail for the want of possession and definite location, if the 6th article of the treaty of December 30th, 1853, ceding this Territory to the United States is considered in connection with this grant, which provides that no grants shall "be respected or be considered as obligatory which have not been located and duly recorded in the archives of Mexico." I have shown ample reason for the filing of the remarkable historical features of the alleged will, said to be the will of the son and heir of the grantee.

Nothing was ever said by claimants under the original deraignment of title that Peralta, the son, had ever made a will, and now that it is produced, and nullifies all of the early deeds of Reavis and and wipes out the other claimants altogether. I likewise show an additional incentative for its late production, which I believe to have been purely an after thought, subsequent entirely to the papers filed in 1883 and claimed at the time as originals.

Even after the execution of the deed to Willing by Peralta, the son, on October 20th, 1864, the copy last filed and referred to above as containing the will of Peralta, the son, makes Peralta execute a codicil on the 9th day of April, 1865, (which would be after the Wickenberg deed to Willing) in the city of Madrid with the stated sole object of granting unto his aforesaid grand-daughter, Dona Sophia Loreta Micaela Maso y Peralta de la Cordoba, the permission legally necessary to enable her to take possession of the grant made to his father in pursuance of the command of his majesty the King of Spain, to his aforesaid grand-daughter "DONA SOPHIA LORETA MACAELA MASO Y PERALTA DE LA CORDOBA, may go and take possession thereof, and in order to secure compliance with this provision I have appointed as her guardian the aforesaid Don Antonio Pablo Peralta."

Reflect on this in the light of the same Peralta having executed a deed to Willing in October 1864, as originally claimed by Reavis. The object of this codicil is to place the present claimant as heir, in a position to take possession of the property, that no one heretofore has ever had possession of, so all important, if contemplated in connection with the treaty of December 30th, 1853. It will be noted that this last will was produced from Madrid, no record being produced from Guadalajara where the record had been bound in books apparently before the necessity for this will was discovered.

To my mind the consideration of these last filed papers go to show against the plausibility of the title as set up by the wife of Reavis, but if, for the sake of argument, we should admit a reasonable appearance of validity of the papers claimed to be photographic copies of originals, I should still report adversely on the grant, as nothing whatever of a reasonable nature has been produced in this office to show that the viceroy ever made a grant to Peralta, or that possession was ever taken of said property by the alleged grantee.

A viceroy was an officer of the greatest discretion and responsibilities and acted at a long distance from the court he was serving, and it is fair to presume was actuated in his acts by his own knowledge as to the situation in the country he was appointed to govern. This must necessarily have been the case (see page 15, section 28, cedula of 1754, Hall's Mexican Law). Much had to be left entirely to his discretion, and the king treating with his subjects domiciled in the country governed by the viceroy, necessitating the action being taken through the viceroy, as a medium, would naturally listen to any reason the viceroy might have for not making the grant, or not performing a certain act and would himself be governed to a large extent by the recommendation of the viceroy pro or con. The very language of the king in his alleged cedula recommending the grant to Peralta is "I, the King of Spain, by this public order, and decree, in conformity with the custom of the Crown, recommend to the most excellent Viceroy of New Spain." etc.

Now there is the plain language of the king (if we accept as valid his cedula) that he only recommends the grant to the viceroy, leaving it wholly and entirely within the discretion of the viceroy to make it or not as would be natural under the circumstances. Did the viceroy make a grant, or did he notify his king that it was impracticable? We are left in ignorance in the premises. Now the claimants allege the viceroy waited ten years and then made the grant. This would only go to show what power he had in the premises; how completely he was master of the situation, and the great discretion he was allowed to exercise by the crown over matters within his own province. He could even allow the king's recommendation to remain unacted upon for ten years. This claim that he delayed action for ten years after the king's recommendation demonstrates the greater necessity of the production of his grant to show that he ever made a grant that was only "recommended" to him by the king.

There are some old books of records of the old mission known as the San Xavier church at present in the possession of one R. T. Hunter, at Washington City, and said to have been loaned him originally by Bishop Salpointe then in control of the San Xavier Mission. These books should have been returned to the proper resting place long ere this, as they are of great importance to many families living in southern Arizona. The claimant Reavis, I presume, in corroboration of the allegations that the church and inquisition were looking after Peralta, had some photographs taken in Washington of what purports to be the sheets of these old books, and filed the photographs in this office. The filing of these photographs as evidence in this case I consider as fatal management on the part of claimants. The photographs filed, purport to show that a copy of Peralta's will and the viceroy's grant, was among the leaves of the old mission books. To my mind the production of these photographs of supposed copies, show to what straits the claimants were driven to obtain corroborating evidence that the viceroy ever made the grant. It is evident the claimants intention to jump up from every conceivable corner something touching on the fact that the viceroy did make the grant, but it seems in poor taste that the old books of the San Xavier Mission, wherein were recorded the births, marriages and deaths of persons under the cognizance of the church, should be selected to have inserted and rudely inserted among its withered leaves a copy of the grant of Peralta by the viceroy, and a copy of Peralta's will. It must be borne in mind that these books have been out of the custody of the church for many years, and that we know very little as to their history in that time. The photographs produced show that what appears to be the regular pages of the old book bear every indication of age, the writing is done with a quill pen, the sheets are regular in shape and size and present an even appearance in matter of age, handwriting, etc., with the exception of the very sheet that the claimant Reavis relies so much on. Here we have a radical change, a complete departure of perspective. In the first place the sheet is pasted in at right angles to the other sheets and is one-third larger than the regular sheets. The upper end of the pasted in sheet is inserted in that part of the binding that holds the back of the large book together, instead of being in regular order, nor is this the only singularity about it. The writing, ink and paper is different from the reaular leaves of the book, the entries proper being in a regular hand, written with a quill pen, and the sheets proper bear an appearance of having been written about the same time, while the sheet pasted in, I unhesitatingly pronounce written with a steel pen, which would, of course, have been impossible if the sheet was pasted in there at the time it was made to appear as the date was fully half a century before steel pens were made at all successful. I am firmly convinced that the sheet referred to was pasted in at a comparatively recent date. It is too apparent to admit of doubt and it plays a sufficiently important feature in this case to account for a necessity for its appearing somewhere in ancient archives, though a most inappropriate resting place is claimed for the paper. The committees in Congress can easily cause the books now in the possession of R. J. Hunter to be brought before them for examination as to the correctness of my conclusion, as Mr. Hunter, their present custodian, is a resident of Washington. This can be done without expense. Mr. Hunter offered his services to show up this fraudulent grant, if paid by the government, but inasmuch as the Peralta claim is without any merits whatever, little or nothing would be gained by paying for information that the congressional committee can so easily obtain without expense.

Herewith is published a letter from C. M. Bell, the photographer in Washington, to the effect that Reavis bought from him (Bell) the negatives from which these photographs of the San Xavier Mission were taken. It is to be presumed from this act that the claimant was not desirous of perpetuating these telltale records.

Herewith is an affidavit of Mr. Frank C. Hise, chief clerk of the office of the surveyor general, setting forth the fact that Reavis was in possession of, and exhibited to him a metal seal, which Reavis boldly claimed was the official seal of the Spanish king, and that the Spanish government had entrusted this seal to him under heavy bonds for its return. Was ever a more preposterous claim submitted for serious consideration? The idea that such an occurrence took place is ridiculous, and entitled to no serious consideration, except to show that according to the allegations of Reavis himself, he was in a position to attach the king's seal to any paper that might be useful to him. The photographs filed in this office of what Reavis claimed to be originals in Spain and filed in support of the claim of the wife of Reavis, show as the most prominent feature, the king's seal; and Mr. Reavis exhibts said seal, which while in his possession, he could use ad libitum, and could easily produce just such papers as his photographs purport to be made from. It seems to me that Reavis in producing this metal seal, and his statements accounting for his being in possesson of it, is one of the worst features in this miserably gotten up land claim. Even if the seal be genuine and the Spanish government did allow Reavis to have it, as he alleges, we can readily see that it might be used for fabricating papers and possibly avoid the detection of the fabrication of the papers better than the finest counterfeit seal could, as its impress would be perfect. Regarding the matter in either light, it is a dangerous instrument to be at large, and should have been kept in Spain, if genuine, and if a forgery should not be in Reavis' possession. The allegations of Reavis in connection with this seal absolutely unsupported by coroborative evidence are too monstrous for the credulity of parties having jurisdiction over private land grants.

Forgery, (Massol Deed).

In the original deraignment of title from the original

grantee to James Addison Reavis, it will be remembered was a deed alleged to have been executed by F. A. Massol, as attorney of George M. Willing, to James Addison Reavis. The Massol affidavits herewith show this deed to be a deliberate forgery. I became convinced of this from the appearance of the face of the deed, and during my former term as Surveyor General, I learned Mr. Massol's address by correspondence, and would have obtained conclusive evidence of the forgery had not my term of office been curtailed by the appointment of a successor. I am satisfied that it was ascertained by the claimant that I had located Mr. Massol, and it was probably understood what my object was in finding him. After I had found Mr. Massol and was in the way of securing the information I wanted, the claimant Reavis disappeared. When he again appeared at this office he said he had spent the intervening time in Madrid, and he presented the entirely new chain of title in his wife, and without showing any particular reason why, he abandoned the chain of title in himself, wherein occurred the forged Massol deed. This deed was originally a bona fide deed for some mining claims executed by F. A. Massol as attorney for Willing, but to some other grantee than Reavis, and all the blank portion of the deed had been carefully red-lined. In a different colored ink from that used in writing the body of the deed and in a different hand writing, Reavis was made grantee, and after the blank space had been used to convey several mines, the blank space not used had been red-lined, showing conclusively that nothing but the mining claims was to pass by the deed; then down below, in the middle of the printed matter, in the same handwriting and ink used in making Reavis the grantee in the deed, this great landed estate was supposed to have passed from Willing to Reavis through the medium of F. A. Massol as attorney, and still several years later Willing himself put papers on file in Prescott showing title in himself. I do not show this forgery in connection with the latest claim that the man Reavis makes through his wife, but to show what means has been resorted to in this case to fraudulently wrest from the domain of the United States an estate large enough to prove a satisfactory principality to the ordinary European potentate.

When Mr. Massol learned of the existence of this fraudulent deal he acted with the greatest promptness in repudiating it

The Granting of Minerals.

One of the most suspicious features of this alleged grant is, that it passed absolute title to all the minerals on the property.

That this was regarded as an extraordinary feature is, to my mind, conclusively shown by the alleged letter of Peralta to the king, Carlos III, asking him to confirm the grant, with the minerals. When we consider that this confirmation was wholly unnecessary at law and that the original grant was made to give all minerals, I cannot but infer that the alleged letter from Peralta to the king asking confirmation, was a cunningly devised plan by some interested party to make up the fatal defect of the absence of the viceroy's grant by showing that Carlos III confirmed the grant papers submitted to him by Peralta and thus made a grant, whether the viceroy had made a grant or not. While this may be an ingenious mode of perfecting title, it has legal defects that would be fatal to such a claim.

The course observed by the Spanish monarch in regard to mineral lands does not admit of belief that he relinquished all minerals in such a vast territory, covering what was then known to be a rich mineral country.

Legal Claimants,

I maintain that there are no legal claimants. No competent evidence to prove that heirs or legal claimants exist, has ever been filed in this office. Under the original papers filed in this office in 1883, by Reavis, by which papers he claimed title in himself as plain "James Addison Reavis," his claim was that the original grantee was in the year 1748 so well and favorably known in Spain, and to the king of Spain that he was selected by the monarch, Ferdinand VI, to be made a grandee of Spain, and to have conferred on him one of the largest estates in the world, certainly the largest in the United States. It would naturally be inferred that Peralta was a man of high station in New Spain, and should have been a very prominent historical character. It was especially recited in the original cedula of Ferdinand VI that this great grant was in recompense for valiant services in war. When we consider the importance of the grant, the title of Baron of the Colorados, and the high reputation the alleged Baron had as a soldier (as established in the cedula) it would be absolutely essential that Peralta should be a historical character, and that the death of so prominent a man should be noticed, but history is strangely silent on this subject, and nothing is established regarding the members of his family.

Bancroft's "Arizona and New Mexico," just published, on pages 398 and 399 publishes an account of the Peralta claim, and deraigns the title to Reavis through Willing; which title Reavis now entirely repudiates, though Reavis was claiming its validity actively enough at the time Bancroft's volume on Arizona and New Mexico was being compiled. Bancroft closes his account as follows: "In a sense the title is plausible enough on its face; but it is somewhat remarkable that annals of the province, as recorded, contain no allusion to Peralta, to the Caballero de los Colorados, or to the Caudal de Hidalgo."

Considering the vast production of papers from archives by Reavis, I can only reconcile Mr. Bancroft's statement on the ground that he is a pioneer investigator and like President Santa Ana, the Mexican authorities, and the Spanish authorities, must have visited the archives before Reavis had been there, which may account for Mr. Bancroft's failure to find the records.

To say the least with such a record he must have been a man in middle life which would date his birth somewhere about the year 1700. In the natural course of events his children would have been born before 1760, and still Reavis tells us in the papers that he originally filed, that the son of the grantee was in the little town of Wickenberg, Arizona, in 1864, where he deeded to Willing, and for aught that is proved to the contrary, may still be living. This state of affairs is highly improbable, if not utterly impossible. If we suppose the Peralta at Wickenberg making the deed to Willing in 1864 was eighty years at the time of said deeding, his father at the time of his birth was certainly in the neighborhood of eighty years of age, and in the natural order of things as they exist in ninety per cent of cases his mother must have been seventy-five years of age at this important epoch in the Peralta family history. The lack, however, to satisfactorily prove any relationship between Peralta at Wickenberg and the old Baron of the Colorados, settles the question of title in this direction, and completely disposes of those claiming under the deed from the Wickenberg Peralta. California and Arizona have many Peraltas. It is a common name and very full evidence would be required to prove a connection between a Peralta in Arizona and the alleged baron.

The claimant under the new deraignment of title is the wife of "James Addison Peralta Reavis." She claims as a lineal descendant of the grantee, but the claim is vague, and not established, even by the papers filed; which would be thrown out by any court as unsatisfactory, Her case has the same remarkable feature of longevity evidenced in tracing the descent through the Peralta at Wickenberg as we are given actual dates. The original grantee in his will as produced by copy from Madrid is made to say under date 1783 that he is 'seventy-five years of age, married to Dona Sophia Ave Maria Sanchez, now residing in Guadalajara　*　　*　　*　　I declare that by my marriage with the aforesaid Dona Sophia Ave Maria Sanchez we have had one son who is called Miguel Peralta de la Cordoba y Sanchez and who is two years of age or thereabouts."

The age of the mother so all important in considering this case is left to the imagination. No papers are produced to prove the date of her birth, but when we are told that her husband is seventy-five old by his own confession, and with nothing to prove an extraordinary difference in their ages, I must naturally infer that she was seventy years old, or thereabouts, at the birth of this child; this is a natural conclusion. Now if the Peralta making the second will defining so particularly the "monumental rock," and the giving of possession, and who made the codicil in Madrid in 1865, be the little two year old boy in 1783, he was 84 years old, at the time of making the codicil, immediately after which he died, as the papers filed show. Satisfactory evidence identifying the Peralta making the second will with the two year old babe of the alleged grantee is not produced, and the entire line down to the present claimant, is unsatisfactory, the whole practical record of the lineage appearing in the copy of the authenticated copy of the will of an alleged Peralta, claiming to be the grandfather of the present claimant, but failing to show in any trustworthy way that he was the direct heir of the grantee, or that he was the same Peralta, who about the same time was deeding the entire Peralta grant away in Wickenberg for the paltry sum of One Thousand dollars, although at that time (1864) Arizona was being settled up, and the value of a great estate, like the one under consideration must have become apparent. If these two Peraltas, the one making a will in 1863, and a codicil at Madrid in 1865 willing away all this property; the other executing a deed at Wickenberg, Arizona, in 1864, deeding away all this property are one and the same man, then which one, if either, is the legal heir? And how can the question be settled without a complete chain of evidence? If they are one and the same person, how can the acts of willing away the property at Madrid, and deeding away the property at Wickenberg to different persons be reconciled? If it was shown that they were one and the same person, and capable of doing so rascally an act as providing in a codicil to his will, to give possession of the Peralta Grant to his granddaughter, the present claimant, when he had a year before at Wickenberg deeded the estate to Dr. Willing for $1000, would he not be scoundrel enough to personate the son of the grantee, and forge his name? And if claimant Reavis alleges these apparently two Peralta's as one and the same person, and the son of the old Baron, then his wife would fare poor as heir, inasmuch as his deeding away the grant to Dr. Willing, a year before the date of the codicil would deprive him of leaving to her the estate already sold. The claimants dare not allege the identity of the two men, and they cannot prove that either is heir. The wife of Reavis is claiming under a Peralta's will and codicil made at San Francisco and Madrid respectively in 1863 and 1865; and the legal representatives of Dr. Willing are claiming under the deed of 1864, executed to Dr. Willing by a Peralta at Wickenberg. Nothing entitled to consideration to prove either title is on file.

Boundaries and Possession.

The only papers on file in this case, to show even approximate location of this grant, are certified copies of authenticated copies of the supposed originals not locatable.

None of the papers in the form submitted to me as evidence, are entitled to be treated as evidence, or worthy of credence. Alleged copies and photographs of crude pen drawn maps, without having been made from surveys, or having established lines or corners or alleged measurements on the ground, as was customary in giving possession of grants under the Spanish and Mexican laws, are not entitled to serious consideration in connection with showing the location of the grant.

This is particularly the case where possession was never taken, nor a reasonable claim as to boundary lines ever established on the ground.

In the middle of the last century "Pimeria Alta" was over run by apache Indians. The apaches were always a warlike, murderous race of Indians, and the whites dreaded them from time immemorial, and very carefully avoided them These are indisputable facts, although Peralta, the grantee, is made to make a rough drawing of 19,200,000,000 square varas of land claimed by him, no claim is made that a survey ever occurred, and it is a fact, that possession was never given Peralta in the customary way which has prevailed in Spain and Mexico for the greater part of the past century, and is so essential in defining boundaries, and locating land, enabling the grantee to comply with the law requiring perfect records of all proceedings in connection with the grant, and its location.

It is claimed that the grantee, Peralta "established the western frontier line thereof, running from north to south to the basin of the Maricopa mountain; to the east of the Sierra Estrella in a direct line to the west of the mouth of the valley of the Santa Cruz, crossing the river Gila and the Salt river, and in conformity with the concession of the viceroy of New Spain, granted under the decree published by order of his majesty, the King of Spain, I send with this an eastern perspective (map) of the tract as described."

This mode of allowing the grantee to locate himself in the manner suggested, would have been a radical departure in the usual proceedings attending the location of Spanish Grants. Such a line might be located anywhere within a territory of a dozen miles in width, even allowing that such a mountain as the Maricopa mountain was known and so designated one hundred and thirty years ago. This line itself would show a degree of uncertainty that would invalidate a bona fide grant for lack of proper designation.

The affidavit of Mr. Monihon herewith, details a conversation, had both with Dr. Willing as to the location of the grant, and also a later conversation had with Mr. Reavis. It shows to a remarkable degree, that they were then claiming this grant as a "floater" and were looking around for a most desirable spot for its anchoring. In corroboration of Mr. Monihon's affidavit, and to show the extreme absurdity of undertaking to positively claim any established, or well defined boundary line, it will be remembered that Reavis originally claimed a certain hill or hills near the line of the Phoenix and Maricopa railroad, as being the Maricopa mountain Peralta described in 1788. Reavis claimed that he was positive of these then selected locations being identically the same spot described by the original Peralta; and he rested his whole claim as to the western boundary on this mountain, and his claim to the other boundaries was dependent on this western boundary as established by him. No hieroglyphics on the rocks figure I in this location; no such remarkable coincidence was ever claimed, as a map, one hundred years old, drawn on a barren rock, which had fallen from its original resting place; but with the ordinary fatality accompanying the remarkable muniments of title in this case, finally landed, map side up, at the foot of the hill.

Later on, however, Reavis discovered, through some means presumably satisfactory to himself, that the initial monument was eight miles south of the spot originally claimed by him. The floating quality of this grant, as evidenced in this change, is accounted for in the affidavit of Mr. Monihon. This change was made by Reavis contemporaneously with the filing of the claim of his wife. Reavis positively asserts to day, that a large rock covered with Indian hieroglyghics, or especially marked for the purpose of this grant, is the initial point; and that the tracings on the rock referred to, form a map of the grant. This state of affairs, it will be remembered, was carefully laid out by the will of Peralta, the alleged son of the original grantee, in the codicil the said son is alleged to have executed in Madrid, although no record of this will or codicil is produced from the proper archives in the United States, where the property is located.

How Peralta, the son, found out so much of his father's doings in connection with this grant, that his father (the original grantee) apparently did not know, is veiled in mystery.

It is my opinion that this conveient will and codicil supplying so many legal deficiencies was produced for the purpose of floating the initial point to a spot eight miles south of its prior establishment to avoid including the property of the Arizona Canal Company, a rich and powerful corporation. (See Monihon's affidavit) which according to the original location was included in the claimed boundaries of the grant. By shifting the initial point, the greater part of the company's property is outside of the boundaries, but the loss to the claimant of this valuable property is more than made up by including the Gila valley in the neighborhood of Solomonville. That Reavis appreciated thoroughly the value of the property added is shown by the affidavits of Mr. Manning and Mr. Hise, herewith. This act in itself shows that Reavis is today, by his own actions, eight miles out in his boundaries, or was under his original claim. If anything could have been added to show the uncertainty as to the boundaries, this act of Reavis' has completed the showing.

The identifying of the rock with the hieroglyphics as the correct initial monument, and which was never in any way referred to by the original grantee, is farcical. Even if we allow that any markings on the rock was not of modern origin, it is nothing more than the ordinary Indian hieroglyphics found on the rocks all over Southern Arizona. I have visited and personally inspected many localities where they occur, and have seen the photographs filed by Reavis of the alleged map on the rock. It is wholly unworthy of serious consideration and could only be entitled to be considered a monument of this grant if corroborative evidence was filed here showing that possession was given the original grantee, and that this identical rock was selected as a boundary monument, and marked according to the allegation of the codicil produced here by Reavis.

It will be borne in mind in connection with this change and the adoption of this rock as a monument, that Peralta the alleged son and heir who made the deed to Dr. Willing at Wickenburg, Arizona, said nothing about any such rock. If Reavis claims that the Peralta who made the deed at Wickenberg in 1864 is the same Peralta who made a codicil in Spain in 1865, then he must have acquired all the information so romantically included in the codicil within a year following his deeding the property to Dr. Willing at Wickenberg.

The last will and codicil produced in behalf of the wife of Reavis will commend themselves as most remakable productions of detailed minuteness of description, and for supplying fatal discrepancies in other papers already filed. The lack of all acceptable evidence to prove relationship between Peralta (who describes the rock, and the hieroglyphics so ingeniously), with the original grantee, if such a grantee ever existed, is a fatal defect and renders all alleged description of location contained in the will of the alleged son of no importance whatever. The Peralta at Wickenberg who made the deed to Willing has as much claim to be the son of the original baron of the Colorados as far as the papers presented here go, as the Peralta making the remarkable will, and a codicil in Spain; and the Peralta making the deed at Wickenberg, Reavis originally claimed, got the papers that Reavis originally filled in this office direct from President Santa Ana, which under ordinary circumstances would seem to give color to the claim that he was the son of the original grantee. Under these circumstances the "monumental rock" is entitled to no consideration. The moving of the location eight miles south shows conclusively that claimants have no knowledge of practical value, either to themselves or to anybody else as to the correct locus of this grant.

If we should admit this grant as legal it is utterly impossible to define even its approximate boundaries. Under no circumstances can it be intelligently located from the papers produced in this office. The land claimed can never be intelligently taken possession of, nor could a deed for a portion of it ever be executed that would have any legal weight.

By their own showing, eight miles is a pretty wide margin for land boundaries.

It has been the custom of Spain and Mexico in investing

titles in grantees to give judicial possession and to make surveys. Lines were frequently marked by natural monuments; if desirable natural monuments could not be utilized artificial monuments of stone were built. The lines were surveyed and measured, sometimes estimated, between natural objects; but in all cases the locating of a grant occurred on the ground granted. When possession was delivered it was done in a manner sufficiently intelligible to enable the grantee to pass title such as a court would recognize. It was then the duty to file the plat of survey, with all the proceedings appertaining to giving possession in the proper governmental archives; as to manner of obtaining grants under viceroys, and the requirements in giving possession (see chaps. V & IX, Hall's Mexican Law). This shows that detailed proceedings such as surveys, locations, etc., occurred on the ground.

The oldest of the Pima Indians located at present in the "Pimeria Alta" of the days of the Jesuits at San Xavier del Bac, whose fathers and forefathers have been born and resided from time immemorial in the immediate country alleged to be covered by this grant, have no knowledge or tradition of such a grant or any one taking possession of such a property and it is almost certain such a tradition would exist if such an occurrence took place as claimed. (See affidavit Hon. P. R. Brady, herewith). Besides this the law of Spain applicable to the time when this grant was said to have been made, anticipated possible trouble with the Indians by providing that they should be consulted and treated with in regard to land grants in their neighborhood, and a knowledge of the transaction of giving this land to Peralta would have been disseminated among peaceable Indians living on the land such as the Maricopa and Pima tribes.

The state of affairs that existed regarding the boundaries of this grant would invalidate it for lack of certainty, if the grant was determined to be genuine. The laches of the original owners receiving a grant in 1758, under a viceroy of

Spain, who neglected taking possession of the property until it passed under the independent Mexican government, and still neglected taking possession until it became the property of the United States by the treaty with Mexico, and who thereafter still neglected taking possession for a period of thirty years, should forfeit every property right. It is preposterous now, for the United States to be asked to put claimants, or alleged heirs into possession, whose ancestors or grantors were unable to produce satisfactory evidence, that they owned this land.

To show how seriously the Mexican authorities considered the question of positive boundaries, I will call attention to the "Buena Vista Grant," which was made in the early part of the present century. In this case the attorney-general reported to the treasurer-general, in the matter of the survey of the grant "that in the measurement made, are only found the measurements made from the center to the east, west, north and south, without making out the square, without which no survey of a Sitio can be considered to have been made," and the papers were returned on this account, the treasurer general having approved the views of the attorney-general.

It is not to be supposed that this extraordinary care sprung into practice at a moments notice, but rather that it had prevailed for fifty years before, and that it was made part of the law of Mexico, on account of its having been the ordinary practice theretofore. In many of the various cases involving land grants, as reported in the U. S. reports. the question of boundaries and taking possession, has steadily arisen, and many grants have been declared void, and of no effect, on account of the lack of documentary proof of possession etc. required by the Spanish and Mexican laws.

Proceedings Required in Granting Lands in 1758.

The Cedula of October 15th. 1754, which will be remembered, was issued between the alleged recommendation of the King in 1748, and the alleged grant by the Viceroy in 1758, somewhat changed the modus operandi, hitherto prevailing in land grant matters. It relieved the grantee from being compelled to have his grant confirmed by the king.

The proceedings for the adjudication of untitled lands customary in 1777, were unquestionably the same as those practiced in 1758, in which year the Peralta Grant is said to have been made.

The proceedings of 1777, are quite minutely stated to have been the following:—

First, Writing of the applicant submitted to the special judge of land and water.

Second, Writ of attorney-general.

Third, Attorney's report, authenticated by notary on what was called "Acordado."

Fourth, Transmission of the "Acordado" to the governor of the province, where application was made.

Fifth, Proceedings (paso) of the lieutenant-general of the province.

Sixth, Proceedings of the justice of the town, where the application was made.

Seventh, Writ of execution.

Eighth, Writ of order to publish warrant.

Ninth, Writ of publication requiring the interested parties to present witnesses.

Tenth, Testimony of witnesses.

Eleventh, Writ to summon the owners of adjoining lands, if there be any.

Twelfth, Summons to same parties.

Thirteenth, Reply to same.

Fourteenth, Appointment of experts.

Fifteenth, Appointment of interpreters.

Sixteenth, Acceptance of the charge.

Seventeenth, Writ to visit place of proceedings.

Eighteenth, Ocular examination.

Nineteenth, Notice that survey and ocular examination had been terminated.

Twentieth, Measurement with cord.

Twenty-first, Beginning of the measurement of the land.

Twenty-second, Continuation of the measurement with cord.

Twenty-third, Notice that measurement had been concluded, and report of the result obtained.

Twenty-fourth, Declaration showing the extent of the land that had been measured.

Twenty-fifth, Map of the land.

Twenty-sixth, Appraisement.

Twenty-seventh, Opinion of the judge of the proceedings, declaring whether there is not prejudice of a third party, and if land can be granted.

Twenty-eighth, The record of the proceedings is delivered under seal to be transmitted to the special judge of lands and water rights, who resides in Mexico.

Twenty-ninth, The special judge ordered the records to be referred to the attorney-general.

Thirtieth, Opinion of the attorney-general of the proceedings.

Thirty-first, Decision of judge, comply with the instructions of the attorney-general.

Thirty-second, The royal officers are instructed to revise the sum for which the land was adjudged.

Thirty-third, Receipt of said sum.

Thirty-fourth, Transmission to the attorney-general for confirmation.

Thirty-fifth, Issue of grant.

(See Mexican ordinances of lands and water rights.)

What Judge Field said on page 261, 4th. Wallace (Graham, United States) is equally applicable to the Peralta claim, under the above required proceedings. Judge Field says:—

"As we have had occasion heretofore to observe, the Mexican law, as well as the common law, made a formal delivery of possession, or livery of seizen of the property, essential after the execution of a grant, for the investiture of the title. This proceeding was usually taken by the magistrate of the vicinage, with assisting witnesses, in the presence of the adjoining land proprietors, who were summoned for the occasion. As preliminary to the actual delivery of possession, the land had to be measured, and its boundaries established, when there was any uncertainty of description of the premises. Various regulations for the guidance in these matters of the magistrates were prescribed by law. That which concerns the present inquiry is that they required the magistrate to preserve a record of the measurement, and all other steps of the proceedings, to have the same attested by the assisting witnesses, and to furnish an authentic copy to the grantee. By this proceeding—called in the language of the country the delivery of juridical possession—the land granted was separated from the public domain, and what was previously a grant of quantity became a grant of specific tract."

As to Records and Where to be Found.

The council of the Indies, "Conseljo Supremo de Indies," was formed August 1st, 1524, and held its sessions at Madrid, Spain, and had both executive and judicial jurisdiction and its powers were exclusive of all others as regards the governmental affairs of New Spain, and it continued the exercise of such powers until the year 1834. See Sec. 6, page 3, Hall's Mex. Law. In Law 43, page 27, Lib. 11, Tit 2, White's recompilation it is provided "No memorial from any person whatever shall be received for services which shall not be supported by certificates from viceroys, generals, or other chiefs under whom such services shall have been performed, except those persons who shall have served in the councils."

Such certificates were to be furnished to the council of the Indies. Peralta was an alleged captain of dragoons, and claimed the grant as a reward for military and other services.

It is postive from the laws existing at the time of this alleged granting of the land to Peralta that the king would not have issued a recommendation to the viceroy of New Spain to make a grant, except through the medium of his council of the Indies, which was made to sit at Madrid so as to be convenient to his royal person, and created especially to take cognizance of such matters, being located near the royal person of the king for easy consultation on matters appertaining to the very country over which the grant was to be floated and preceding any action by the king or council, the proper certificate as to Peralta's services would have to be produced and would be on file in the archives of the council.

The law 54, page 29, White's Recompilation provides, "and we permit that in cases of petitions and memorials for rewards or for compensation for services *or other matters of grace*, the same may be entitled to consideration and reconsideration, the records whereof and all matters connected therewith shall remain in custody of the secretary of the council, together with the other papers of the office."

Now the grant to Peralta would be purely a "matter of grace" to reward him for military or other services of a distinguished nature, and the records of the proceedings should be in the place provided by law. The records of the council of the Indies should show all the details of the steps preceding the grant, if such a grant was ever made, and under the law the viceroys recommendation in favor of Peralta or the recommendation of some general under whom Peralta served, should be on file in the records of the council of the Indies, as the very initial step of the whole proceedings. Nothing of this nature is produced. No one can reasonably dispute that it would be especially fitting that a matter of so much importance within the jurisdiction of the viceroy of New Spain should have been recommended by him (especially when the requirements of the law are considered) and it is hardly probable that the king would make a recommendation in the absence of so important a link in the routine observed at time and in the face of all the laws established by himself, even if he meant to override the council of the Indies in this single instance. No recommendation from the viceroy in favor of Peralta on which the king could base his act is found but in lieu of such proper procedure the king is made to take the initiative on an alleged recommendation of the Inquisition etc. which never had any jurisdiction whatever, and is not produced. Such an act would have been to completely ignore the viceroy under whose jurisdiction Peralta and his great estate would come. Such a state of affairs cannot be entertained, but if under the circumstances the king was to violate the established custom of the time we imagine it would be for some grandee of Spain close to the throne and would not occur in the case of a man wholly unknown to Spanish history. The action of the king in 1748 is alleged to have occurred "Agreeably to the petition of the Royal Inquisition of New Spain, the recommendation of the Council of Commerce, and the Judge of Appeals," still these papers are not even produced from the archives of the council of the Indies where they should be found.

The Law—Lib. 11, Tit. 2, Law 45, White's Recompilation provides: "The party addressing a memorial shall therein set forth all the services rendered by him up to its date, because no other shall thereafter be admitted and the members of our Royal Council of the Indies shall receive orders not to admit them."

Now it is only claimed that Peralta was a captain of dragoons and operating in the province of the viceroy, therefore if a person memoralized the king to perform an act of grace, and make a grant to Peralta, the memorial would be minute in setting forth the services of so small an officer as a captain of dragoons, who expected so vast a grant, and more especially when an ocean lay between the king and the brilliant performances of Peralta, and without the recommendation of the viceroy.

History and the records however are silent in the matter and the kingly act is left in solitude. While the jurisdiction of the Council of the Indies comprehended small matters of reward, compensation and grace, they likewise took cognizance of matters of the greatest importance occurring in the Indies, and New Spain, wherein the kingdom of Spain was interested and no difficulty should exist in producing the proper records appertaining to the alleged grant, if bona fide. That the author of the paper produced here as the act of Ferdinand VI, whether king or layman, understood thoroughly what an important factor the Council of the Indies was in the premises, is evidenced by the reference in the cedula to persons, etc., who recommended the grant to the king, in the apparent hope that sight would be lost of the proper channel through which a grant of the nature of the Peralta grant would have to go.

"The council to have supreme jurisdiction in the Indies to make laws, examine statutes, and to be obeyed there, and in these kingdoms." Lib. 11, Tit. 2, Law 2, White's Recompilation. "No council, chancery tribunal, judge, no justices of these kingdoms other than the Council of the Indies, shall take cognizance of affairs connected with them." Lib. 11, Tit. 2, Law 3, White's Recompilation.

I quote these laws to show how completely the affairs of the Indies were in the hands of the council in 1748, and prior to that date, and how exceedingly improbable it appears, that the king should ignore that body, in the matter of a mammoth grant; to a mere Captain of Dragoons 3000 miles away. Law 42 provides: "In the reports made to us in cases of rewards, and compensation for services the qualifications, merits and services of the persons in whose behalf they are made, shall be fully stated, together with the testimony and the facts supporting the same, setting forth how and where such services have been rendered, the compensation made in money or otherwise, and the objections of our fiscal, if such there be; and for the better fulfillment of this, there shall be in the custody of our secretaries, a record and statement of said compensation, and reward as shall have been granted by us, and each shall keep one for the provinces and districts resorting to this office." This law shows conclusively that the greatest care was exercised by the King of Spain, in making grants, and rewarding persons. He had to have evidence of just what the services were, and how much the petitioner for further royal favors had received, in order that he might judge whether the money paid, or favors done, had been adequate compensation for the services performed. In no other way could royal patronage be safely bestowed, and papers would have been produced in the case of such a grant as that alleged to Peralta, showing everything connected with his services, before the king would act, otherwise Peralta might have been unwisely rewarded in the premises. The Audiencies of the Indies, were under the jurisdiction of the supreme council of the Indies. See Lib. 2, Tit. 15, Law 1. Consequently all proceedings had before them, would be referred with the evidence to the council of the Indies; which shows an additional reason, why the full record of the preliminary proceedings of the Peralta Grant, if genuine, should be found in the Archives of the Indies.

The following is a legal factor in the Peralta grant, of no mean proportions: See Lib. 2, Tit. 15, Law 164. White's Recompilations. "The audiencies shall besides keep a register, where shall be inscribed the names of the inhabitants of their respective districts, a statement of their services, and the amount of compensation paid to each in money, by the way of extra compensation, or otherwise, and of the offices to which he has been appointed, which register shall agree with the journal of the audiencies, in order, that whenever a claim for services shall be presented, said audience may set forth its opinion thereon. Of this register a copy shall be transmitted to our royal council of the Indies, with as little delay as possible, and if subsequently there be made to it any addition, correction or amendment, information thereof shall immediately be transmitted to us, that the corresponding alteration may be made in the copy first sent, and that we may know what is the nature of the services, and grant the proper compensation." This shows how particular the provisions were for transacting business in the Indies of the nature of the

Peralta Grant, and all kindred acts. Here we have as careful a system of registration, as the present laws provide for in our own country.

"The audiences shall besides keep a register, where **shall** be inscribed the names of the inhabitants of their respective districts, a statement of their services." How in the face of such laws, could so exalted a personage as Peralta have been entirely unknown? The presumption is greatly against his having existed or having received a grant.

In the view that the Peralta grant is claimed as an absolute grant in consideration of services rendered, and that no further proceedings after the grant was actually made were to occur, the records should have been complete, and when I say records, I refer to the records of the Council of the Indies. It is utterly impossible for such provisions of law as existed at the time the grant is alleged to have been made, to have been ignored, and the archives should be replete with records connected with the Peralta grant, if ever made.

In Pico vs. **U. S. 2nd** Wallace 282, Judge Field in delivering his opinion said: "As will be perceived from this statement it was an essential part of the system of Mexico to preserve full record evidence of all grants of the public domain and o the various proceedings by which they were obtained. When therefore, a claim to land in California is asserted under an alleged grant from the Mexican government reference must, in the first instance, be had to the archives of the country embracing the period when the grant purports to have been made. If they furnish no information on the subject a strong presumption naturally arises against the validity of the instrument produced which **can** only be overcome, if at all by the clearest proof of **its** genuineness, accompanied by open and continued possession of the premises."

Now the **above** unquestionably not only **contemplates** the production of full records, but it contemplates **these records** being produced from the proper archives, that is the claimants to the Peralta grant should have produced full records from the archives of the Council of the Indies. *The proper archives of Spain,* "embracing the period when the king's recommendation purports to have been made," *were the archives of the Council of the Indies.* According to Judge Field then inasmuch as proper records have not been produced in evidence from the proper resting place, a strong presumption naturally arises against the validity of the instrument produced, and the Judge goes on to say that the clearest proof must be offered as to the genuineness of the papers accompanied by open and continued possession.

The claimants of the Peralta claim fall short in both these requirements.

The Pico case covered a claim alleged to have been granted under the regulations of 1828, which were adopted in connection with the colonization law of 1824, but what was applicable in the Pico case was equally applicable in the Peralta case, as far as record evidence of the grant was concerned, as the laws governing in the premises in the time of the council of the Indies were equally circumspect in prescribing the necessity of perfect records of grants. Judge Field, in the Pico case, says: "Tested by this rule, the grant under which the appellant claims was properly rejected as invalid."

It is provided in Lib. 2, Tit. 33, Law 1, White's Recompilation that when anyone asks for reward he shall go before the Royal Audience of the District, set forth his claim, etc. The audience then to seal the same together with their own opinion in the premises and send it through two different channels to the council of the Indies. This gives additional force to the wisdom of the court's position in the Pico case, as applied to the Peralta case; and on the question of the nonproduction of the records from the proper archives, this case must fail, if all else is admitted as genuine.

To the student of Spanish law it early becomes a patent fact, that during the previous century and prior thereto, the royal patrimony was the beneficiary in all cases of grants of land belonging to the throne, but in Peralta's case the king recommends to the viceroy the absolute donation of the 5,000,000 acres of land, in violation of all former customs and existing laws, and all this to a mere captain of dragoons in New Spain. The objects of the Spanish grants were to encourage settlements. To extend the lines of civilization throughout the length and breadth of Spanish provinces. To settle up the countries as rapidly as possible in order to be able to offset the incursions of hostile Indians. Conditions were inserted almost without exception in grants to incur the settlement of a certain number of familes, or people, on the land granted within a certain limited time; as in the case of "Arrendonda." See page 691, 6th Peters. Or mills were to be erected, towns to be built, cattle to be put upon the land, or some other requirement as would conduce to advance the state of civilization. See U. S. vs. Clark, 8 Peters, page 436; U. S. vs. Sibbald, 10 Peters, page 313; U. S. vs Mills, 12 Peters, page 215. This class of grants cited above made with conditions precedent in the early part of the present century, do not seem to have grown out of any royal order, but became customary in the interest civilizing the American provinces. I quote these cases in the interest of showing that so well were the king's desires in the premises understood, and so thoroughly were precedents established that without any royal order on the subject the governors, captains, generals and others empowered by the king to act inserted conditions precedent to grants, and they stood in that condition when the territory was acquired by the United States. Dozens of these grants with conditions, as the only cost of purchase or gift will be found in the United States supreme court reports. All these grants, however, were Lilliputian when compared to the great grant to Peralta, and we are told that this unknown; insignificant captain of dragoons, got his grant without conditions or any formalities of law whatever; while Bancroft tells us on page 360, volume 9 that Augustin de Ahumada y Villalon, the viceroy, who is alleged to have made this 5,000,000 acre grant to Peralta who was appointed viceroy by the king on account of his great military career in Italian wars, died without any means and left a poverty stricken widow, is it reasonable to believe that the king would leave this great historical figure to die in poverty, this sub-king of the Spanish realm, and still regard this man Perlta with so lavish a hand, *when he is not even mentioned by the Audiencia of his own district*, under the law, and reward him by violating established laws and customs and sacrificing the opportunity to enrich the royal coffers; all of which is incredible, considering the date at which the grant is alleged to have been made.

Bancroft particularly speaks of the enriching of the king by Augustin de Ahumada's predecessor, and it is not consistent that this marked departure should occur in the case of a man like Peralta, who was not known, and whose name was not even among the records wherein were registered the most humble *under the laws of that time*.

One of the weakest propositions in the case is the production of the papers purporting to be from the archives of the holy inquisition. A knowledge of the Spanish law appertaining to the times under consideration shows that there is no more propriety in producing the Peralta records from the archives of the inquisition, than there would be in producing the present records of the state department from the archives of Trinity church 100 years hence. The inquisition, under the law, was not the proper custodian for land grant papers, and in no way, shape or form had jurisdiction to mix up in the matter, and it is very unbecoming, from a legal standpoint, to produce records from such alleged resting places.

The king zealously watched and controlled his New Spain provinces through proper established channels, and left the inquisition to successfully perform its proper functions; the disseminating of the religious doctrines of the times, etc., throughout the country entrusted to their spiritual care by the Spanish government.

The papers of testators etc., have on all occasions provided that no bonds shall be required of executors in this Peralta claim. It is a fact that an executor executing so important a trust as settling up this vast estate, would probably be required to furnish bonds in the sum of at least $10,000,000 so a very potent reason for the insertion of so important a clause as the exemption from bonds exists. Very few persons indeed could furnish bonds to administer an estate of this kind.

One very noticeable feature in this case is that no will is produced in this office enumerating that the testator owned a watch, money, heirlooms, or even books, carriages, or that inseparable companion to the average Mexican a horse. In the will of the grantee, in 1783, and the codicil of 1788, not a thing is devised but the Peralta grant. Are we to be asked to credit a showing that a grandee of Spain, a man of heroic deeds, and recognized merits, a man under the immediate patronage of a great king, a friend of a viceroy, and a captain of dragoons possessed nothing in the world that he could leave his child except this very land claim, which it is so essential should be traced in these wills.

Again in the will and codicils of the alleged son we have a repetition of the same state of affairs. The son had lived a long life, had been in Mexico and the United States, and when he died with a great flourish of will and codicil, he left the Peralta grant to his alleged grand daughter, the present claimant, and did not as much as leave a finger ring in addition. This identical Peralta claim is the whole subject of both the wills and codicils of these great men. Neither of them had a house, corral, or a head of stock, but the *Peralta grant* is never lost sight of and as a solitaire its effulgence is undimmed by less kingly associates. If Peralta ever lived on this grant in possession, where is the house and other property that should be noticed in the will?

It will be remembered that at the date of these wills and codicils the great industry of the Mexican land owners was the raising of cattle and exporting tallow and hides. A grandee of Spain of the importance of Peralta and with the advantages of a captain of dragoons, owning 5,000,000 acres of land should have had cattle on a thousand hills, but by the wills and codicils filed here by this man Reavis he did not possess at the time of his death a calf, sheep or goat. Neither did the old baron, nor his alleged son leave either a working interest in mines or mineral wealth of any kind unless we except those on their alleged grant. When we consider these facts and at the same time consider the fact that they never had possession of the alleged grant, nor derived any benefits from it, they must indeed have been poor.

Such an inconsistent state of affairs is wholly unworthy of credit, and shows to my mind the fabrication of these papers by a person or persons of shallow reasoning powers.

In the brief submitted by the Hon. Clark Churchill, herewith, will be found a careful criticism of the Spanish used in the several documents filed in this case, and a comparison of the Spanish used in the documents, purporting to be of the same origin, but produced from different places. Many variations in spelling etc., are found, and the class of Spanish used is not at all times of the high order that was used in the Castilian court of the last century. Other matters of importance are touched upon by Mr. Churchill in his brief; of value in the consideration of this case.

I think I have conclusively shown that this Peralta claim to a very large part of this territory is worthless from a dozen legal standpoints, the chief of which is that *no grant was ever made by the viceroy,* as alleged. When such gigantic efforts are made to produce evidence, and records as we have witnessed in this case, without locating the grant by the viceroy, it is to my mind positive, that no such grant exists or ever existed. The papers in the case read like a romance, and to believe in the claim we have got to discredit the representations of our minister at Madrid and the Mexican government, who caused thorough searches to be made of the archives of Spain and Mexico, without finding records, and we are compelled to credit the story that the king departed from his own laws, the established customs of the times and overriding all precedents at a break neck gait, undertook to reward a man with a veritable principallity, whose name is unrecorded in history, and of whose brilliant deeds in war there ceases to be a remembrance.

If these allegations are true as to the king's act, is it to be wondered at, that the viceroy failed to credit such a state of affairs on the part of the king, and ignored a recommendation, which after all, submitted the matter to his discretion?

The claimant in alleging that the viceroy made a grant asks us to believe that in his zeal to serve Peralta he departed from the long established customs of New Spain, and waived every precedent and law in favor of Peralta. But if we believe all this the claim would still fall for legal reasons.

Another ridiculous feature in this claim is the allegation that the papers, not even claimed as originals, were gotten together and sent to Carlos III for confirmation by Peralta. *The cedula of Oct.* 15*th*, 1754, *relieved solicitants for titles from transmitting them to the king for confirmation, on account of great expense.* Why should Peralta have sought the confirmation of the king on *August first* 1768, and incurred this heavy expense, when this alleged grant specifically carried minerals? No reasonable answer can be given this state of affairs.

Herewith are letters from Spain showing conclusively that the search of that government was in vain. A very long letter furnished Mr. Morgan, our American minister to Mexico, by the secretary of state in charge of the department of foreign relations of Mexico, dated Mexico, June 14th, 1884, being an answer to questions emanating from this office during my former term says: "It appears that under date of December 6th, 1883, and at the request of Mr. Hopkins it pleased you to have the same identical search made by the employees of this office for the purpose of exhibiting to the interested party the documents he desired to examine regarding concession, Mr. Hopkins said in his petition quoted in the order referred to that he had in his possession a copy with the seal of the inquisition and certified by the secretaries of the tribunal, Mess. August Anthony Carrillo y Callautes and Joseph de la Ceda y Debago, and also by Mr. Joseph de Avalas, notary.

He solicited permission to examnie the original signatures

of King Carlos III, and the archives of the viceroyalty of 1758, and also the archives and the seal of the royal tribunal of the inquisition of the year 1777. The search being made at the time, and repeated today, no record has been found relating to the said grant, under the following headings: 'Grants,' 'Lands,' 'Royal Decrees and Internal Provinces,'"

"Mr. Hopkins was shown various printed signatures of King Carlos III as no original ones are on file, the seals of the inquisition, and he was informed that there was no record of such grant. The search having been repeated as aforesaid, to comply with the request made by Minister Morgan, in the name of the government of the United States no better result has been obtained."

Then follows the matter which is corroboration of the powers of the council of the Indies, historical matter, etc. Now it is distinctly alleged that this is a viceroy's grant, and still the archives of the viceroyalty itself at the City of Mexico, show not a scratch of a pen in relation to this grant, although thorough search has been made twice on requests from this office, and it is explicitly stated above, that not only has the archives of the viceroyalty been searched but the viceroy's archives *of the very year* in which the grant is alleged to be made. Is this not conclusive evidence that the viceroy never made a grant? Santa Ana's alleged letter says: "*He searched in vain.*"

This question was put to the Mexican government: "Was any record kept in Madrid of the concessions made by the viceroy of New Spain, on the recommendation of the king of Spain?"

In this same letter the answer comes as follows: "Undoubtedly such record was kept in the archives of the Indies, as it is generally known that the viceroy reported his most ordinary acts to the king."

Where are the records of the council of the Indies and why are they not produced? Where too, is the record that should have been produced from Madrid, showing that Carlos

III, confirmed a grant, which by the cedula of 1754 did not have to be confirmed?

The same letter again says: "As in the present case it is alleged that the grant made by the Marquis de las Amarillas, to Mr. Michael Peralta in 1758, was confirmed by King Carlos III in 1772, it is safe to presume that not encountering in this office the royal decree conveying the said confirmation, it may be found in the archives of 'Simancas' which contain those of the Indies, accumulated during the time of the viceregal government, and which pertain to the country formerly known as New Spain."

Now we have *"Simancas"* the place of deposit of the archives of the Indies. Unfortunately for claimants during my previous term I caused these archives to be searched, and the letter herewith from Hon. Dwight T. Reed, to Secretary Bayard, March 26th, 1885, shows that *the search failed as usual.* What can be made of all this except that no such grant ever existed?

The royal supreme court of Guadalajara had power to make grants of land, and was in direct correspondence with the king. Such grants as were made by the powers immediately referred to should properly be of record at Guadalajara; but claimants do away with all such considerations as it is positively asserted that this grant was made by the viceroy and it falls on that issue. The archives of the viceroyalty were in the City of Mexico where he presided. *A president of the royal audiencia presided at Guadalajara.*

The letter under consideration contains the following: "It is probable that under the archives of the Indies now kept at Simancas in Spain a record may be found of the documents called for, in view of the fact that even *the most ordinary acts were reported* explicitly to the king of Spain by the viceroys, especially so when in the present case a special mandate of the sovereign had issued previously."

This letter is from the archivero of the general public archives of the nation of Mexico, a savant of Spanish laws, customs and regulations. To argue the illegality of this grant further, with such a showing as I have made. I consider a loss of time, but one more point in this report before I rest. The following question was asked by this office of the Mexican government: "What rule appears to have been observed in Mexico at the time the document above referred to is said to have been executed. Were the original concessions, recommendations, etc., filed as records or copies of the same? Did the government put on file the originals or the copies? Did grantees receive the originals or copies of the same?"

The archivero answering in the letter under consideration says: "The viceroy and the royal supreme court generally made the grants of land and water rights in the name of his majesty, the king of Spain. keeping a certified copy on file in the section of grants, and the original document was delivered to the interested party as a safe guard for his title."

I now ask the claimant or claimants to produce this original grant of the viceroy.

Speedy and final action should be had on this base claim in order that the people of this territory may enjoy their homes with peace of mind. And parties guilty of forgery or the fabrication of papers that have caused so much trouble should be vigorously prosecuted by the government, and that without delay.

I recommend that the alleged grant should not be confirmed as is prayed for, it being to my mind without the slightest foundation in fact and utterly void.

Respectfully submitted,
[Signed]   ROYAL A. JOHNSON,
U. S. Surveyor General for Arizona.

Affidavits and Letters Referred to in Report.

LEGATION OF THE
UNITED STATES OF AMERICA.

MADRID, 6th, June 1884.

ROYAL A. JOHNSON, ESQ.,
U. S. SURVEYOR GENERAL,
Tucson, Arizona.

SIR:—Referring to your letter of the 1st, February last to Mr. Foster relative to the "Peralta Grant" and to his reply of the 4th April, I have now to enclose herewith, a copy of a letter of the 14th ultimo, addressed to me by the Sub Secretary of the Ministry of Ultramar, from which you will observe that *careful search has been made for the desired documents but without success.*

The Department of State, at the instance of the Secretary of the Interior, has sent me a copy of your letter to him dated March 14th last. Upon the receipt of the photographs therein referred to the Legation will request the Minister of Ultramar to cause a further search to be made.

I am, sir,
Your obedient servant,

[Signed]   Dwight T. Reed,
                        Charge 'd'Affaires ad interim.

P. S. I beg to add that Mr. Foster first applied to the Minister of Fomento *who replied* (after Mr. Foster had left for the United States) *that the desired documents did not exist in his department* and recommended that we apply to the Minister of Ultramar. This I did with the above result.

MINISTRY OF ULTRAMAR

DEAR SIR:—The Chief of the General archives of the Indies in Seville, in a communication of date the 3d instant, informs me among other things as follows:

"Dear Sir:—(Hino Sr.) This office has duly received

your communication of the 24th of April last, enclosing a copy of the royal order communicated by his Excellency the Minister of Ultramar, that the certified copies desired by the government of the United States be made of all existing documents relating to a concession of land situated in the Territory of Arizona, known as the Peralta concession and particularly of a recommendation made by Ferdinand VI December 20, 1748, of the concession granted by the viceroy of New Spain, D. Augustin Ahumada y Villalon, Jan. 3d, 1758, and of the confirmation of said concession by Carlos III, Jan 20th, 1776.

I at once arranged that the sixth official, the oldest in the office and not one who was less fitted to guarantee the success of the search, should proceed immediately with it.

For the past four days he has devoted himself exclusively to the search *without any success whatever.*

That which by royal order has been communicated by the Minister of Ultramar I transmit to you as an anwer to the B. L. M. of your Excellency of date April 22 last requesting to know if the documents mentioned in the memorandum you sent enclosed existed in the archives of this office.

God protect your Excellency many years.
Madrid, May 14th, 1884.
      Sub Secretary,
        Miguel Sanrez Vigul,
To the representative of the United States of America.

    DEPARTMENT OF THE INTERIOR,
     GENERAL LAND OFFICE,
    Washington, D. C., Jan. 24th, 1885.
Royal A. Johnson, Esq.,
 U. S. Surveyor General,
  Tucson, Arizona.

SIR:—For your information I herewith transmit the following described papers, viz:

Copy of a letter from the Hon. Secretary of State to the Hon. Secretary of the Interior, under date of the 12th instant with a copy as its enclosure, being a copy of a communication dated Dec. 24th 1884 from the Legation of the United States at Madrid, to the Department of State, relative to the alleged "Peralta Grant" pending investigation in your office.

Please acknowledge the receipt.

Very Respectfully,

[Signed]
Two enclosures.

N. C. McFarland,
Commissioner.

DEPARTMENT OF STATE.

Washington, D. C. 12 Jan. 1885.

The Hon. H. M. Teller,
Secretary of the Interior.

SIR:—Referring to your letters of the 30th July and February last, I have the honor to enclose a copy of a dispatch from Spain touching the Peralta grant, Arizona Territory.

I have the honor to be, sir,

Enclosure, Mr. Reed,
to Mr. Frelinghuysen,
24 Dec. 1884, No. 272.

Your obedient servant

Fred'k T. Frelinghuysen.

LEGATION OF THE UNITED STATES.

Madrid, 24, Dec. 1884.

No. 275.

The Hon. Fred'k T. Frelinghuysen,
Secretary of State.

SIR:—Referring to the Department's instructions Nos. 129 and 224, and to Mr. Foster's reply No. 262, I have the honor to enclose herewith a copy of the reply of the Sub Secretary of Ultramar to Mr. Foster's application in the matter of the "Peralta Grant."

It will be observed from the letter of the Sub Secretary that the *original copy of the Peralta Grant does not seem to be among the archives of the Indies at Seville*, but there is a similarity between the signature of Carlos III, attached to other documents on file there, and that, as shown in the photograph forwarded with your No. 224, the chief of the archives at Seville reports, however, that the original document may possibly be found among the archives at Simancas. I have consequently requested the Minister of Fomento under whose department the archives at Simancas come to be good enough to cause a search to be made for the original document and to aid in the search. I have sent him the photograph above referred to which was returned to me by the Sub Secretary of Ultramar.

With a view to complying with your instruction No. 283 I have requested of the Minister of State a photograph of the autographic signature of Carlos III, and the Minister has replied by note dated the 19th instant that he has referred the request to the Superior Chief of the Palace.

I have etc.
Dwight T. Reed.

DEPARTMENT OF STATE'
Washington, D. C., April 16th, 1885.

The Hon L. Q. C. Lamar,
    Secretary of the Interior.

Sir:—Referring to the letters of your department of the 30th July last and February 1884 I have the honor to enclose a copy of a dispatch from Spain additional to the one sent your department on the 12th January last touching the Peralta Land Grant and a fac simile of the autograph of Carlos III, of Spain received therewith.

I have the honor to be, sir,
Your obedient servant,
T. F. Bayard.

Enclosures,
Mr. Reed to Mr. Bayard, 26th March, 1885, No. 316.

No. 316.

LEGATION OF THE UNITED STATES.
Madrid, 26th March, 1885.

To the Honorable T. F. Bayard,
    Secretary of State.

Referring to Department's instruction No. 283 and to my

reply No. 275 I have now the honor to enclose herewith a fac simile of the autograph of Carlos III, and of a copy and translation of a note from the Minister of State transmitting the same to me. As will be observed by the note of the Minister the character of the document would not permit of a photographic copy being taken.

With further reference to my No. 275 I beg to state that I have received a note from the Minister of Fomento enclosing to me the reply of the *Director of the Archives at Simancas* stating that careful search had been made and that the so called *"Peralta Grant" does not exist among those archives.*

I have the honor to be
Very respectfully etc.
Dwight T. Reed.
[Translation.]

Enclosure No. 3 to Mr. Reed No. 316.

MINISTRY OF STATE,
Palace, 13th March 1885.

MY DEAR SIR:—In reply to your note of 13th of December last, in which you request in the name of your Government a photographic copy of the signature of King Carlos III I have the honor to inform you that his Majesty, my August Sovereign, deigned to accede to the request but the character of the documents from which it had to be produced not permitting it to be done photographically he ordered a faithful fac simile of the autograph to be made, which I enclose to you.

I avail myself of this opportunity to reiterate to you the assurance of my distinguished consideration.

J. Eldnayen

Mr. Charge 'd'Affaires of the United States.

LIBRARY OF CONGRESS,
Washington, August 13th, 1889.

Hon. Royal A. Johnson, U. S. Surveyor for Arizona,
Tucson, Arizona :

DEAR SIR:—In reply to your communication of July 29th last, to Hon A. R. Spafford, Librarian of Congress, which has been forwarded to me by him from Mohawk, New York, where he is spending his vacation, I have to report that although I have not found in this library any Spanish book printed either in or out of Spain, in exactly the year 1748, there are many published in neighboring years. I have examined a considerable number of them, and it appears to me that the printing in the photograph you send is more modern than that in them. The long "S" except as a final letter appears to have been used invariably until up to say, 1770, but that is not found in the photograph. All the letters in the latter, even when not differing much in form from the old ones, seem to be more clearly cut, and rather in more modern style. All the indications point to its being at least some what later than 1748.

Very respectfully,
C. W. Hoffman, for
A. R. Spafford, Librarian of Congress.

[Copy]

PORTRAITS OF NOTED MEN.
ENGRAVING,
PHOTOGRAPHIC ARTIST.
C. M. BELL,
Nos. 459, 461, 463 & 465, Penn'a Ave.
Washington, D. C.

Crayons and
    Pastel Portraits.

Washington, D. C., Sept. 25, 1889.

R. A. Johnson,
    Surveyor General, Tucson, Arizona.

DEAR SIR:— In reply to yours of Aug. 29th in regard to photographic copies for Mr. Reavis, would state that we photographed them and sold him the negatives several years ago but kept no record of them.

We only keep a record of those we retain.

Very resp'y,
[Signed]   C. M. Bell.

Phoenix, Arizona, August 20th, 1889.

To his Excellency
    Governor Lewis Wolfley,
        Phoenix, Arizona.

DEAR SIR:—Pursuant to your request I have the honor.

to submit herewith the following sworn statement of what I personally know of the claim of one James Addison Reavis, to the so-called "Peralta Grant."

With much respect,
Very obediently yours,
James D. Monihon.

Territory of Arizona, } SS
County of Maricopa.   }

James D. Monihon, being duly sworn, deposes and says. I am a resident of Phoenix, Maricopa county, Arizona, 53 years of age, have lived in Arizona nearly all the time since 1863.

In the winter of 1866 and 1867 I became acquainted, in Prescott, Arizona, with one Dr. Willing, he was a mining man, and claimed to have mines in Black Cañon, to the southward of Prescott. I kept a livery stable and he used to put up his horse there. I was keeping the stable for a man named Alexander.

Doctor Willing asked me if I knew a man by the name of Peralta, and if so, if he was not in Black Cañon. I told him that I knew the man but that I believed that he was at Wickenberg. Doctor Willing then asked me if I knew of any one that intended going that way as he would like to have company as the Indians were very bad. I told him I knew of two or three men who were going that way in a day or two; he left with them. I cannot now remember their names. I did not see or hear of him again until the fall of 1867 when he came to a stable I was keeping for myself on Plaza at Prescott. I kept his two horses there until his bill ran up to some $35.00 or $40.00 and he said he wanted to go to St. Louis on some business and would send me the money from there. I told him I couldn't let him go in any such way; that he would have to have the money before he left. Next day he came to me and said he had a fine scheme on hand; that he had got a floating grant; that he would sell me one half of it for two hundred and fifty ($250.00) dollars down and we could lay it on those mines and plains where the grass was growing in abundance. The two hundred and fifty dollars cash down, the balance when we sell the land, but he never named any amount or what the balance would be. I felt very indignant over it, and answered him very shortly saying I didn't want to take any land away from my neighbors, that I didn't believe in grants, and thought they were all fraudulent; he endeavored to reason with me, saying it was an easy way to to make money if properly carried out; that we could sell the mines back to the owners, and take our pay as they took it out of the mines, and in the valleys we could keep large herds of stock, and sell the beef to the miners, and the people who would come into the valleys.

Finding no encouragement from me, he sold his horses, paid my livery bill, and went off on a government outfit. I could not say now just what kind of an ou'fit it was he left on for New Mexico, saying that once in New Mexico, he could get all the help he wanted, to go through to St. Louis.

Before he left Prescott, when the people there found out about his claims to a pretended grant and his intention to try to float it over their lands they got hostile, and treated Dr. Willing in such a manner that he became alarmed, and said to me that he believed that he would try to float it over the Hualapai valley, and leave Prescott out, and asked me about the valley. Next I heard of Dr. Willing he came to Prescott and recorded his grant claim, and that night he died there. This was in 1875 or 1876.

In the spring, I think in March 1877, James Addison Reavis came to Phoenix claiming to be agent, I think, for the Alta California, a San Francisco paper. I was keeping a livery stable at that time in Phoenix, Arizona. He wanted me to take him out over Salt River Valley so that he could write it up. I drove him out some four or five miles west. He was very much pleased with the valley and inquired very particularly about the junction of the Gila and Salt rivers, and wanted to know if the ground at the junction of the two rivers was solid, and as it was stone, and had been practically unchanged for ages, I told him so. I told him that about half a mile back from the junction of the rivers was a solid formation of rock. We wound our way in a north western direction over the valley for a couple of hours, but nothing more was said about the river.

Upon our return home we came to a river about three miles northwest from town. We stopped to view the surroundings, and he told me that he could get a floating grant and thought he would lay it on this valley and thought he would make his initial point at the junction of the Gila and Salt rivers. I told him that he had not better try to float any grant on this valley, as the people would hang him. He said he was going to do it to make money, and the Southern Pacific Railroad Company would back him. He had passes to travel on the Southern Pacific Railroad wherever he wanted to go. He was short of money and had been compelled to walk from a station on the railroad to Phoenix, and his feet were sore, and he had the appearance of being worn out. I may be in error in the date or year of his coming to Phoenix as above described; but the statement given is exactly what occurred when he came. He left for Prescott, and I was informed that he could not pay his bill at the hotel in Phoenix to Charles Salari. I understand that he went to Prescott to try to get the papers on this grant. I think he told me he had an order for papers that were in Prescott. Afterwards he came to Phoenix and claimed to have a grant and it was the same one that Dr. Willing had been endeavoring to lay. He recorded a lot of papers in connection therewith.

Last year in May, 1888, while I was on the train coming from St. Louis to Arizona, I met Reavis. We had quite a conversation on general topics. He referred to the so-called Peralta grant, and said that the line of it was now two miles north of the city of Phoenix, that he had moved the south line of his grant eight miles further south. I asked why, and if he was afraid of the Arizona Canal Company, and if they were too strong for him to fight on the grant claim. He said yes, and that he wanted to take in Florence and other locations that he considered more valuable; and that he had relocated his initial point at the point of the Maricopa mountain about eight miles from the junction of the Gila and Salt rivers, on a rock bearing hieroglyphics. Since then I haven't seen him.

James D. Monihon.

Subscribed and sworn to before me this 20th day of August 1889.

P. K. Hickey,
Notary Public.

[SEAL]

State of California, }
County of Santa Clara, }
and town of Los Gatos. }

F. A. Massol being first duly sworn says that the deed of mining claim and landed property as recorded May 24th, 1883, at request of Wells Fargo & Co., which said deed conveys unto J. A. Reavis the above mentioned property in Arizona, and bears date of acknowledgement of May 22, 1867, was recently exhibted to him, and after careful scrutiny pronounces it a forgery as regards the grantee. That to the best of his recollection he does not know to whom he conveyed the mining property. That he did not know nor had he ever heard of J. A. Reavis in 1867, nor did he afterwards until after the death of George M. Willing which occurred in 1874, or 1875. That to the best of his knowledge the said J. A. Reavis obtained the deed aforesaid from among the private papers of the Willing estate about 1881, in his possession. That he never until recently heard of the land grant recited in the said deed. That that part conveying the land together with all that part granting the described property unto J. A. Reavis has been inserted since the deed left his possession.

     [Signed]   F. A. Massol.

Subscribed and sworn to
this 14th of September 1889.

A. Berryman,

[SEAL]   Notary Public.

State of California, } ss
County of Santa Clara. }

Fen Massol being first duly sworn says that during the years of 1880, 1881 and 1882 he was a resident of the city of Sacramento, county of Sacramento and State of California, and that during that time he met and became acquainted with J. A. Reavis. That he has seen the deed purporting to convey certain mineral and other lands in the Territory of Arizona to the said Jas. A. Reavis, dated May 22, 1867 and executed by F. A. Massol, his father.

That he fully believes the said conveyance was obtained from his father in the month of July 1881 when the said Jas. A. Reavis secured a number of private papers relating to the estate of G. M. Willing, Jr., in Arizona. That to the best of his knowledge and belief the said deed was made and executed to an unknown party and conveyed nothing but mineral lands. That the said deed never passed from the possession of his father until the before mentioned time. That to the best of his knowled and belief the said deed has been changed and the name of J. A. Reavis inserted in the place of the original grantee, and all that part deeding lands of Miguel Peralta has been inserted since the death of G. M. Willing, Jr.

That the said deed was executed under a power of attorney of Geo. M. Willing, Jr.

Los Gatos, Oct. 3rd, 1889.

[Signed] Fen Massol. [SEAL]

Subscribed and sworn to
before me this 3rd day of October 1888.

A. Berryman,
[SEAL] Notary Public.

Frank C. Hise being first duly sworn deposes and says that he is a resident of Tucson, Territory of Arizona. That he is at present and has been for a period of nearly four years chief clerk of the office of the Surveyor General for the district of Arizona, and deponent further says that he knows one James Addison Peralta Reavis, and that soon after the return of the said Reavis from Madrid, he exhibited in the private office of the then Surveyor General Hise, a metal seal weighing about one pound which he claimed was the Spanish King's seal, the same as the photographic copies filed in the Surveyor General's office on Sept. 2nd, 1887, by said Reavis showing the impressions of. Said Reavis was questioned as to how the royal seal was allowed in his hand by the Spanish government. He responded that he had to give heavy bonds for the safe keeping and return of the seal.

Frank C. Hise.

Sworn to before me this eighth day of August, 1889.

Royal A. Johnson,
U. S. Surveyor General.

[SEAL]

Levi H. Manning being first duly sworn deposes and says: That he is a resident of the city of Tucson, Territory of Arizona. That he has been mineral clerk in the office of the United States Surveyor General at Tucson, and that he was employed in such capacity during the year 1887, Deponent further says: That he is personally acquainted with a man representing himself to be James Addison Peralta Reavis, the claimant of an alleged land grant in Arizona, designated as the "Peralta Grant." That at or about the time the said Reavis saw fit to move his initial monument south about eight miles from the point originally claimed by him as the original point (center point of the west boundary line) I heard him in conversation in the Surveyor General's office say that the change of location would very materially enhance the value of the grant as it would take in Solomonville and the rich Gila valley in the neighborhood of Solomonville; also valuable lands in the Santa Cruz valley, and further deponent saith not

Levi H. Manning.

Sworn to before me this eighth day of August 1889.

Royal A. Johnson,
U. S. Surveyor General.

[SEAL]

Frank C. Hise being first duly sworn deposes and says: That he is a resident of the city of Tucson, Territory of Arizona. That he has been chief clerk in the office of the United States Surveyor General at Tucson and that he was employed in such capacity during the year 1887. Deponent further says that he is personally acquainted with a man representing himself to be James Addison Peralta Reavis, the claimant of an alleged land grant in Arizona, designated as the Peralta Grant.

That at or about the time said Reavis saw fit to move his initial point south about eight miles from the point originally claimed by him as the original point (center point of the west boundary line), I heard him in conversation in the Surveyor General's office say that the change in the location would very materially enhance the value of the grant as it would take in Solomonville and the rich Gila valley in the neighborhood of Solomonville also valuable lands in the Santa Cruz valley and further deponent saith not.

Frank C. Hise.

Sworn to before me this eighth day of August 1889.

Royal A. Johnson,
U. S. Surveyor General, District of Arizona.

Territory of Arizona, }
County of Pinal. }

Be it known that on this day personally appeared Peter R. Brady a citizen of Arizona Territory resident of Florence, Pinal county, who being duly sworn deposes and says: That he has at different times within the last two or three years had conversations with several of the principal Indians of the Pima tribe, living upon the lands embraced in the Gila valley, and now claimed by one J. A. Reavis and associates as their property, under title from the Spanish government made more than a hundred years ago, and that said Indians have upon every occasion stated that to their positive knowledge no such claim or grant has ever been made, and moreover that the Spanish government, and afterwards the government of the Republic of Mexico had always protected them in their occupation of said lands, and at different times paid them annuities in the way of clothing and money and that from time immemorial they have been recognized by said government as the rightful owners of said lands. Peter R. Brady.

Subscribed and sworn to before me this 5th day of October 1889 and my official seal affixed. G. H. Oury,
[SEAL] Notary Public.

Department of the Interior, before the Surveyor General of the United States in and for the Territory of Arizona, at Tucson in said Territory.

In the matter of the claim of one self styled Sofia Loreta Micaela de Maso Reavis and James Addison Reavis.

Now on the twenty-fifth day of February A. D, 1889, appeared before the Surveyor General of the United States in and for the Territory of Arizona, Thomas H. McMullin, who was thereupon duly sworn to testify in the above entitled matter to the truth, the whole truth and nothing but the truth, and examined as a witness by Clark Churchill, Esq., counsel for settlers on the lands covered by the claim, and testified as follows, to wit: My name is Thomas H. McMullin; I reside in Phoenix, in the Territory of Arizona. In the winter of the years 1887 and 1888 I was in the City of Washington, D. C. While in said city of Washington during said winter I saw and examined the original book, photographic copies of parts of which have have been filed in this office by the claimant herein, or one James Addison Reavis, her reputed husband, and which book is claimed to be an original book of the records alleged to have been kept at the Mission San Xavier del Bac by the Jesuit fathers. This book was then in possession of one Hunter, a resident of the City of Washington. I fully identified the book as being the same as that which was photographed and the photographic copies of parts of which are on file in this office in this matter and designated by claimant as exhibit 1, 2, 3 photographic copies of records of

San Xavier Mission. In the printed brief and argument of petitioner filed herein, I observed that the sheet or page of said book upon which this writing appears whereon the petitioner relies as referring to the pretended grant, is of a different kind of paper from that in the other pages of said book, and said page or sheet so relied on by petitioner clearly appears to have been interpolated and inserted into said book at some time after said book had originally been bound. The paper composing said sheet was of a different size from that of the other pages of said book; so that when the book was closed the outer edges of the paper was folded into the book to prevent it from protruding beyond the edges of the other leaves of the book. The writing on this sheet ran vertically across the page at right angles with the writing on the other pages when the book was opened in the usual manner. The writing on the other pages ran horizontally across the page in the usual form of writing in books of record. The other parts of this book seemed to be composed of ancient paper. This sheet had evidently been so inserted in said book after said book had been bound and was composed of paper of an entirely different kind and manufacture, and was comparatively new and not of the ancient character as that forming the other parts of said book. The writing on the other pages of said book was evidently done with quill pens, but the writing of this said sheet had evidently been done with a steel pen. The dates of the several entries in said book appeared to be consecutive in chronological order from time except as to the entries on this interpolated sheet. The entries and writing on this interpolated sheet are not in said chronological order. The dates written on this interpolated sheet are later in time than the dates of entries which are made upon the other sheets and pages of said book which follow it in said book. Said Hunter, in whose custody said book was when I saw and examined it claimed that it was the original book of records which had been kept at the Mission of San Xavier del Bac by the Jesuit fathers, and that the photographic copies of parts of the same had been taken since said book had come into his possession, and he stated to me that said sheet of paper had been inserted into said book since it first came into his possession, and while it was temporarily in the care of James Addison Reavis, one of the claimants herein who had borrowed said book from him—said Hunter—in the year 1882 by misrepresentation and deceit, and kept it for three (3) days and that during said time there was inserted into it the sheet containing the entries relied on by the claimants in this matter, and said Hunter further informed me that within a few days after returning said book said Reavis appeared before him and produced his photographic copies of parts of said book, similiar to those filed herein, and demanded that he —said Hunter—should certify to their correctness, but that he—said Hunter—refused to make any certificate on account of said fraudulent interpolation. The above and foregoing testimony having been given by the witness Thomas H. Mc-Mullin at the time and place and before the Surveyor General as above stated but not then taken down nor reduced to writing, the same is now here written out in full correctly on the foregoing pages and reverified by the said witness who has signed his name hereto and who does hereby certify that the above and foregoing is a correct transcript of his testimony.

[Signed]   Thos. H. McMullin.

Subscribed and sworn to before me this 12th day of October, A. D. 1889, And I certify that Thos. H. McMullin is the identical person referred to in the foregoing transcript.

                               J. H. Carpenter,
[SEAL]   Notary Public·

Department of the Interior, Before the Surveyor General of the United States in and for the Territory of Arizona, at Tucson in said Territory. In the matter of the so-called Peralta Land Grant claim.

Hon. Lewis Wolfley, being first duly sworn, testified as follows:

Question by the Surveyor General—What is your name and occupation?

Answer—My name is Lewis Wolfley, and I am the governor of the Territory of Arizona.

Question by the Surveyor General.—Do you know R. F. Hunter, who resides at 225 East Capital street, Washington, D. C. ?

Answer.—I do.

Question by the Surveyor General.—Have you ever had any conversation with him regarding the so-called Peralta Land Grant Claim?

Answer.—I have,

Question by the Surveyor General.—Will you please state in full any conversation you have had with Mr. Hunter in connection with this claim?

Answer.—I was in Washington during the spring of 1889 and met R. F. Hunter, and conversed with him about the Peralta claim. Hunter stated to me that he knew it was a fraud, and that if he was retained he would show that it was a fraud. He further stated he had possession of the old record books of the San Xavier Mission, and that some time ago he loaned them to one Reavis. That after Reavis had possession of these books he returned the same to Hunter, who on examining the books discovered that a sheet of paper had been surreptitiously inserted in the book, relating to the Peralta claim. Mr. Hunter told me he would make an affidavit to this effect.

[Signed]   Lewis Wolfley.

Sworn to before me this fifteenth day of October 1889.

Royal A. Johnson,
U. S. Surveyor General for the District of Arizona.

Notarial Record of the Forged Deed.

Herewith is the notarial record of the *at present changed deed* as it originally appeared (by which Reavis originally claimed the Peralta grant) taken by J. W. Brumagin, notary public of San Francisco, Cal., from the records of F. J. Thibault the deceased notary before whom the forged deed was originally acknowledged by F. A. Massol. The deed at present reads: "This indenture made the twenty-second day of May A. D. one thousand eight hundred and sixty-seven, between F. A. Massol of the city and county of Sacramento and state of California, party of the first part, for George M. Willing of the Territory of Arizona, by virtue of a general power of attorney dated May 11th, 1864 and J. A. Reavis of the second part."

According to the record the deed originally read "Between F. A. Massol of the city of Sacramento and state of California, party of the first part, and *George M. Willing of the Territory of Arizona, of the second part.*"

The deed itself plainly shows on its face where the word *"and"* was erased and the word *"for"* inserted, then all that part in the deed as it now appears after the words *"Territory of Arizona"* was deliberately added to the deed to fit an old power of attorney from George M. Willing to F. A. Massol dated May 11th, 1864, and for the purpose of making the title in Reavis to complete his original chain. It will be borne in mind that Reavis had possession of Dr. Willing's papers. Even the power of attorney alleged to have been executed by Willing to Massol dated in 1864 was never acknowledged by Willing but it was left until March 12th, 1883, and was then acknowledged by one of the witnesses. At this date Willing's papers were accessible to claimant Reavis.

Whatever may be the status of this power of attorney as to its validity is unimportant as the deed was forged to fit it.

Royal A. Johnson,
U. S. Surveyor General.

State of California, }
City and County of }
San Francisco }

I, J. W. Brumagim, a notary public in and for said city

and county residing therein, duly commissioned and sworn do certify that the following:

1867 May 24.		W. H. Allen to George M. Willing, Deed May 22—67 $500 Bradshaw Dist. to John P. Logan, Power of At. May 22—67,
	Pen'y, Ariz. Pen'ny, Ariz.	F. A. Massol to George M. Willing Deed May 22—67 $500 Bradshaw to John P. Logan Power of At. May 22—67.

Is a full, true and correct copy of the record from the book of F. J. Thibault a notary public, now in my possession. Done at the request of Fen Massol.

In witness whereof I have hereunto sent my hand and affixed my official seal at my office in the city and county of San Francisco State of California this twenty-fifth day of October, A. D. 1889.   J. W. Brumagin,

[SEAL]   Notary Public.

Argument of Clark Churchill Against the Claim.

DEPARTMENT OF THE INTERIOR.

BEFORE THE U. S. SURVEYOR GENFRAL FOR ARIZONA.

In the matter of the claim of one self styled Sofia Loreta Micaela de Maso Reavis and James Addison Reavis of lands under the pretended "Peralta Grant."

I

The burden of proof is upon the claimants. They must show to the satisfaction of the Hon. Surveyor General:

1st. That a grant was in fact legally made to Miguel Peralta.

2nd. That they (the claimants) are the owners of that

grant. I take it forgranted that the foregoing propositions will not be denied by any one.

II

No legal evidence has been presented tending to show that any such grant was ever made, and of course, if no grant was ever made to Peralta, then all the claims and pretences of these claimants to the effect that first one of them had acquired Peralta's alleged title by mesne conveyances, and of the other that she is the lineal descendant and sole heir, and hence inherited the title, go for naught, and the investigations of the papers offered in support of those pretences become material only in so far as their inconsistencies and fraudulent and spurious character throw light upon the character of these claimants themselves.

The following recapitulation, analysis and comparisons of the documents presented in this case by the claimants will show the absurdity and groundless character of this claim.

Ex. A is a pretended printed cedula of the King of Spain Fernando VI, supposed to be dated and made Dec. 20th, 1748, pretended to have been presented to the "Cama del Real Santo Tribunal de la Inquisicion de Mexico."

Then follows the pretended report of the Inquisitors to the viceroy, dated at Mexico Oct. 10th, 1757.

This report is to the effect that "Francisco Paner" (the true name being Paver) of San Javier's Missions Padre Garcia, another missionary and the Bishop of Nuevo Mexico, Tameron, have given testimony "That they have no interest in the concession, and that said concession is quite popular and caused many friends among the Pimas and we have determined to recommend the granting of it."

These priests could very well say they had no interest, since by law the ecclesiastics were then prohibited from taking up land.

Then follows a general pretended approval of the grant describing it as being of 300 square leagues, to enclose the Gila river, which concession shall be located to the north of San

Javier in Pimeria Alta in the Vireyno of New Spain, and to include rivers, minerals, etc., etc., signed by *Augustin* de Ahumada y Villalon. Marquis *de* Amarillos, dated Jany. 3, 1758.

Then follows a pretended order or direction to Peralta and to Father Paner (Paver?) to locate the concession as commanded; this is signed only with a flourish or pretended rubric.

Then Peralta locates in a general way his concession, and adopts a *plano* or map of it. (In printed copy this is dated 13 May, 1758. In the testamentary document there is no date.) Ordered, signed and sealed by Peralta, in the presence of Paner, and the witnesses Vega and Galvez.

Next comes a pretended petition of Peralta to the King Carlos III to confirm the grant of Fernando VI, which is followed by a pretended short assent of confirmation, dated Jan. 22nd of 1776; signed by the king and countersigned by Antonio Ventura de Taranco, and directed to the Holy Inquistion of Mexico of New Spain.

This Ex. A was filed in this office March 27th, 1883. Next of the photograph and documents filed in this office Sept. 2nd, 1887.

This photograph, supposed to be taken from an original copy found in a will of Peralta, in the archives of a notary public—now deceased—differs from the Ex. A having a whole sentence more and several words added into the document. Again it has some words less than Ex. A. Hence it cannot be said that either is a copy of the other.

Both documents contain apocriphal words, or in other words they make use of language which was not in use in 1748 and some which are not and never have been Spanish.

I will now note some of the various differences and mistakes and errors of language which appear to me, viz:

1st. Ex. A lacks the following words on the 3rd. line after "cuidad de Mexico Por cuanto, en atencion a los meritos y servicios, por tanto mando al Commandante General" also the words "Capitan de Dragones." Which are contained in the photograph.

2nd. The expression "Por parte de Senor" found in both

the photo and Ex. A was not Spanish in 1748, nor has it ever been to this date; the true expression is "Por Parte Del Senor."

3d The phrase "Fueron aprobodas" is not Spanish: it should be "Que Fueron Aprobadas", this mistake is made in Ex. A and in photograph. This error would not be made by any person who was born a Spaniard, it is only possible to be made by a foreigner, and neither the King nor any of his ministers were foriegners in 1748.

4th In Ex A is found the expression "Fuero Militar," which is proper, but in the photo. this appears as "Fuero Tribunal." There is no such thing known in Spain or Mexico and how it was possible for Somodeville to present to the King such a document to sign is hard to conceive.

5th. In both copies is found the phrase "y para la recompensa de grandes y valiosos servicios, tambien *para* el modo de conducir prontamente las batallos importantes en el servicio del Rey."

Here the word *para* should be *por*. The mistake is very commonly made by Americans speaking Spanish.

The last part of the sentence "en el servicio del Rey" is good Spanish, but very contrary to the habit of the Spanish monarchs, and there is not a single cedula, where, in speaking such a phrase it is not rendered so, "en mi servicio."

6th. "Yo el Rey por este mandato y decreto publico." This phrase, though not very bad Spanish, is contrary to all customs of the kings of Spain in making their cedulas. There is not one cedula where the king repeats his name in the middle of the body of it, or that he uses "este mandato y decreto publico" because the kings of Spain were so strongly impressed with their power that they considered their every word a supreme law; they knew that a cedula was a law and they needed not to say "this public command" or any other expression to increase the force of the cedula.

7th. "Recomiendo el exmo." is bad Spanish; it should be "Recomiendo al exmo."

8th. "Seran Situado" found in Ex. A and photograph. If this sentence refers to *leguas* it should be "Seran Situados."

If it refers to the concession it should be "Sera situada" as it is here it is a verb and participle neither of which agrees with each other or with the subject. This mistake would not have been made even by the illiterate portion of the lowest Mexican people; and such is only possible to a foreigner who stammers Spanish, let alone the king of Spain.

9th. "Y ser tal forma," is not Spanish; it should be "y ser de tal forma."

10th. In Ex. A, "que no molesto," in photo. "que no moleste."

11th "Exmo Virrey de Espana" in Ex. A; in photograph "Exmo Virrey de Nueva Espana."

12th. "Sin embargo incluir" is not Spanish, it should be "sin embargo que incluyan." This mistake is found in Ex. A and Photo.

13th. In Ex. A "Declara el titulo" in Photo. "Declaro el titulo."

14th. In Ex. A and in Photo. the ending is "Asi lo proveyo, mando y firmo."

15th. The king commenced speaking in the first person and ends in the third person. But the use of the words "proveyo mando y firmo" are not used in a single cedula of the kings of Spain from the time of Ferdinand and Ysabella to the revolution of 1820. They never admonish the person addressed that they so "provide, command and signed" but occasionally they end their cedulas thus, "por ser asi mi voluntai" because such is my will. See Pandectas Mexicanes, V. III, page 534 to 536, Cedulas of 1746 and 1805.

17th. The seal in Ex. A was not in use in 1748.

18th. The authentication in Ex. A is contrary to the customs of the times in 1748. In all the cedulas I have examined up to 1810 after the signature of the king "Yo el Rey" is written "Por Mandado del Rey" or "Por Madado del Rey nuestro Senor" so and so is the name of the Secretary of State.

The expression "I the minister so and so put the great seal of state" is not found in any documents of state or cedulas of the kings of Spain up to 1800.

"El sello Real" was in use sometimes, that is "the royal

seal." The great seal of state is borrowed by the concoctor of these papers from his English legal knowledge.

19th. In both Ex. A and Photo. is found an entry beginning with "visitaron y refrendose etc., etc." The whole sentence is barbarous and incomprehensible to Spanish speaking people, but the claimants pretend that it means that "this grant was examined and countersigned in the chamber of the Holy Royal Tribunal of the Inquisition of Mexico, for proofs of claimants to previous grants." The absurdity of this will appear when it is understood that this statement is very cooly signed by Somodeville, who at the time is minister at Madrid in Spain, not in Mexico at all.

If anybody had to sign this statement it should have been the grand inquisitor of Mexico and his secretary.

Both Ex. A and the Photo. are made up in a form entirely different from any cedula of the kings of Spain. The Spanish used is a barbarous jargon, and has more of the English idiom and construction than of Spanish language. The mistakes above pointed out are but a part of those it contains. The author of this cedula appears to have been an American speaking bad Californian Spanish of the present day.

The claimant first presented in 1883 Ex. A as an original copy of the first autograph copy of the King Fernando VI, which having been passed upon by the inquisition, the viceroy and had been taken possesion of by Peralta, this identical printed copy Ex. A is claimed to have been presented to King Carlos III when this king writes this remarkable sentence on it:

"Passo ante mi
fecha en Madrid
a dos de Decembre
de mill setecientos
y Setenda y dos.
    Yo el Rey.

Countersigned by his secretary's signature, Taraneo.

It is very remarkable that Taranco, who for many years served Charles the III as prime minister, in the short sentence above written, "Passo ante mi" etc., etc., should have made three mistakes. I will translate it.

"Passed before me
"dated in Madrid
"the second of December
"of one thousand seven
"hundred and seventy
"two.   I the King."

The unfortunate Taranco wrote passo instead of *"paso"* with one single s; he wrote Decembre when the real Spanish is *"Diciembre"* and wrote mill when it should be *"mil"* with one l.

But what is still stranger is that when Somodeville wrote the original cedula he had also two l's in mil, that was fourteen years before.

By looking at the very bottom of the Ex. A the acknowledgment of the receipt of the cedula by the viceroy of Nueva Espana, is also afflicted with weak knowledge of Spanish, and contains this expression, viz: "Passo mi," by which we who speak English translate it thus: "it passed me." But as a Spanish phrase, the word *passo* should be paso; that is, one s, and accent on the *o*; and the preposition *por* should be between the two words, that is, "Paso por mi," though even such an expression was improper for the case.

For this reason I say that the author of Ex. A was an American who spoke bad Spanish.

In the certificate of Lancaster, appears the word "Mandato." This word was never used by any secretary of the King of Spain, in any cedula up to 1815, when the use of cedulas was discontinued, the only word used was "Mandado,"

We have the following facts evidently apparent from Ex. A.

1st. The type in which it is printed is modern.

2nd. The language is not Spanish and would not have been produced or written by any person acting as amanuensis to the king in 1748 or 1776.

3rd. The seal of the king it bears had not been cast and

was not in existence in 1748, nor in 1772 nor in 1776, according to my information.

Yet King Charles III says in the first page of Ex. A "*passo ante mi, etc.,* Dec. 2, 1772, and signs it '*Yo el Rey.*"

The inference is plain, either King Carlos III arose from the dead to sign in our day, or some person speaking bad Spanish forged his name.

The same hand who signed the king's name in the first page, forged Charles III's name on the last page, pretended to have been done in 1776.

By an examination it is apparent even to the inexperienced that both the signatures of Charles III are tracings; and that the many writings in Ex. A, pretended to have been done at various times and by different persons in it, are the work of the same hand.

Take for instance the expression: "Passo mi" at the bottom of the first page supposed to have been done by Juan Francisco de Guemes, Viceroy of Nueva España about 1749-50.

Then take the "Passo ante mi" supposed to have been written in 1772 by the secretary of the King Charles the III.

Then take the "Passo ante mi" 4th page signed by a supposed original signature and flourish of Joseph Avalos and of Agustin Ant. Cauxillos.

All these passos have the same orthographical mistakes, the two *s s*, and the same character of hand writing,, supposed to have been written by different persons at various times between 1748 and 1772.

This Ex. A purports to be a copy of the original cedula and to contain a copy of the proceedings to execute the will of King Fernando VI. The two last pages pretend to be an original petition of the Caballero de los Colorados to Charles III to confirm his grant.

Then follows the pretended genuine confirmation by Charles III with his genuine signature countersigned by the secretary Taranco, and then it says:

"Al Real Santo Tribunal de la Ynquisicion de Mexico de

Nueva Espana" which means "To the Royal Holy Tribunal of the Inquisition of Mexico of New Spain."

All of which signifies that this instrument, after being sanctioned by the king, was returned by the king to the Inquisition; that the instrument, executed and delivered, should be there kept as a testimony of the fact that it had been so executed. Therefore if this instrument really bears the signature of King Charles III, it has no business in the hands of the claimant, but it should be deposited in the archives of the old Inquisition in Mexico, who are the lawful keepers of it, and its date of filing should be noted in the proper book.

This instrument, if found in said archives, might be presented here in the form of a copy of it, duly authenticated by the keeper of such records, and then it would have a standing before the government of the United States for considation.

As the case now stands, this Ex. A appears as a dislocated fragment from the parent source; and what that source is should be proven first by the claimant against the government of the United States and why or how it came into the claimant's hands without due authorization.

An attempt is made to authenticate this Ex. A by a pretended certificate signed by President Santa Ana, at the bottom of the last page, but it is so blotted and torn that it is impossible to make out what the purport of the authentication is. It appears to be a private letter of Santa Ana without having the countersign of the minister of foreign relations or the seal of state of the Republic of Mexico.

Santa Ana does not say either that Ex. A is a copy or an original or that there is any record of said instrument in any archives of Mexico.

Nor is President Santa Ana the proper person to say the document is a copy of anything in the archives of Mexico, because, though president he is not the keeper of any archives, and his declaration would not be proof of such fact. Nor was it within the scope of the duties or customs of the president of

Mexico to sign in any way any authentication of this character. The practice was for the keeper of the proper archives to certify them, and for the secretary of state, with the seal to certify to the official character of the keeper.

To more fully illustrate the inconsistency of the several documents filed in this office, which are alleged to prove that a royal cedula was made by Ferdinand VI, the following copies of each are so arranged in parallel columns as to show at a glance the difference between them. Of course if they all relate to the same act of King Ferdinand they should be all precisely alike. The column at the left contains the copy found in the pretended will or testament of the alleged Peralta; the middle column, the printed copy and the right hand column the copy in the photograph.

TESTAMENTARY CEDULA.	PRINTED CEDULA.	PHOTOGRAPHED CEDULA.
El Rey Virrey Governador y Capitan General de las Provincias de Nueva Espana y Presidente de mi Real Audiencia que reside en la ciudad de Mejico:	El Rey Virrey Governador y Capitan General de las Provincias de Nueva Espana y Presidente de mi Real Audiencia que reside en la ciudad de Mexico.	El Rey Virrey Governador y Capitan General de las Provincias de Nueva Espana y Presidente de mi Real Audiencia que reside en la ciudad de Mexico: Por cuanto en atencion a los meritos y servicios por tanto mando al comandante. General
por parte de Senor Don Miguel de Peralta de la Cordoba Capitan de dragones conforme a la suplica de la Ynquisicion Real de Nueva Espana y la recomendacion del consulado y Jues de Alzadas fueron aprovadas por ese Govierno y llevadas a la junta General militar y en acuerdo de juicio por conciliacion del Fuero Tribunal y en consideracion y para la recompensa de grandes	por parte de Sr. Don Miguel de Peralta de la Cordoba * * * * * * conforme a la suplica de la Ynquisicion Real de Nueva Espana y la recomendacion del consulado y Jues de Alzadas fueron aprovadas por ese Govierno y llevadas a la junta General militar y en acuerdo de juicio por conciliacion del Fuero Militor y en consideracion y para la recompensa de grandes	por parte de Senor Don Miguel de Peralta de la Cordoba Capitan de dragones conforme a la suplica de la Ynquisicion Real de Nueva Espana y la recomendacion del consulado y Jues de Alzados fueron aprovadas por ese Govierno y llevadas a la junta General militar y en acuerdo de juicio por conciliacion del Fuero Tribunal y en consideracion y para la recompensa de grandes

SURVEYOR GENERAL'S REPORT.

y valioras servicios tambien para el modo de conducir prontamente las batallos importantes en el servicio del Rey: Yo el Rey de Espana por este mandato y decreto publico en conformidad a los costumbres de la corona recomiendo el exmo virrey de Nueva Espana en mi nombre ortorgai y conceder al Sr. D. Miguel de Peralta de la cordoba Medida Comun trescientas leguas cuadrados o dies y nuevo mil Docientos millliones varos cuadrados de tierra seran situado en septentrionales del Vireino de Nueva Espana y ser tal forma que no molesta concessiones anttes, sin embargo incluir todos las tierras aguas y corrientes * * todos las minerales y todas otras coras pertenecientes: y declaro el titulo honorable del Sr D Miguel de Peralta * * * * ser caballero de los Colorados con Grandeza asi lo proveyo, Mando y firmo fecha en Madrid a veinte de Dicimbre de Mil setecientos y cuarenta y ocho Fernanlos Yo el Rey con subrica sello de Espana Por manda to del Rey muestro sr yo ministro y decano del consejo de estado he anotado. aqui el Sello Grande de Estado D Jose de Carvajal y Lancaster.

(2nd Forgery.)

y valioras servicios tambien para el modo de conducir prontamente las batallos importantes en el servicio del Rey: Yo el Rey de Espana por este mandato y decreto publico en conformidad a las costumbres de la corona recomiendo el exmo Virrey de * * Espana en mi nombre otorgai y conceder al Sr. Don Miguel de Peralta * * * Medida comun trescientas lezuas cuadrados * * * * * 19,200,000,000 varas cuadrados de tierra seran situado en septentrionales del Vireino de Nueva Espana y sel tal forma que no molesto concesiones antes, sin embargo incluir todas las tierras aguas y corrientes * * todos las minerales y todas otras coras pertenecientes: y declara el titulo hono rable del Sr Don Miguel de Peralta * * * * ser caballero de las Colorados * * * * asi lo prove vo, Mando y firmo fecha en Madrid a veinte de Diciembre de Mill y setecientos y cuarenta y ocho * * Yo, el Rey * * * * * Por Manda to del Rey nuestro Sr yo ministro y decano del consejo de Estado he anexado aqui el Sello Grande de Estado Don Jose de Carvajal y Lancaster.

(1st Forgery.)

y valioras servicios tambien para el modo de conducir prontamente las batallos importantes en el servicio del Rey: Yo el Rey de Espana por este mandato y decreto publico en conformidad a los costunbres de la corona recomiendo el exmo Virrey de Nueva Espana en mi nombre otorgar y conceder al Senor Don Miguel de Peralta de la cordoba Medida *comde Castillon* trescientas lezuas cuadrados o dies y nueve mil Docientos milliones varas cuadrados de tierra seran situado en septentrionales del Vereino de Nueva Espana y ser tal forma que no moleste concesiones antes, sin embargo incluir todas las tierras aguas y corrientes y todos las minerales y todas otras coras pertenencientes: y declaro el titulo hono rable del *Senor* Don Miguel de Peralta de la Cordoba ser caballero de las Colorados con Grandeza asi lo prove yo, Mando y firmo fecha en Madrid a veinte de Dicimbre de Mill y setecientos y cuarenta y ocho * * Yo el Rey * * * * * * * Por Manda to del Rey Sr *Senor* yo ministro y decano del consejo de Estado he anotado aqui el Sello Grande de Estado Don Jose de Carvajal y Lancaster.

(3rd Forgery.)

The foregoing parallel copies: the printed, the photographed and the testamentary cedula filed in this office present a Darwinian development towards the perfection of the forgery though the successive corrections are not always an improvement on the printed copy, which was filed first.

For instance, the printed copy contains the words "Fuero Militar" which are very proper. The other copies make it "*Fuero Tribunal*" a barbarism having no meaning in the Spanish language. Notice the word "Molesto" this word is tonnd in the printed copy as "molesto" which translated means "I molest," in the testamentary copy it is rendered "Molesta" which means "he molests," and the last development is found in the photo thus "*Moleste*" which means "that he may not molest." This is an improvement, for it means "that the concession may not molest" other concessions.

The printed copy has the word "declara" "he declares," a very improper expression for the king to use, as he commences speaking in the first person; but the other copies mend it by putting the proper tense "declaro" "I declare."

It is evident that when writing the pretended will of el Sr. Don Miguel de Peralta y Sanchez, Ex. A is the instrument alluded to as the original, as appears by examining article 6th of that testament, as it refers to it, beginning with the frontice page thus a cross, red sealing wax, and a piece of white paper where appears to have been a seal. Libro que solo sirve de apuntar etc., etc., and so it goes on to describe minutely the printed copy with every flourish and pretended seal on it, only that a few words are added or changed with or without success to better the meaning of the cedula.

In the printed cedula and in a corresponding place in the statement or copy in the testament of Peralta y Sanchez we find in the one these words, "del padre Exmo Sr Tameron Obispo de Nuevo Mexico". In the testament this is rendered so, "del padre exm Sr Tameron Obispo de Guardiana, y Culiacan y Nuevo Mexico."

The persons who are supposed to speak here are the grand inquisitors, ecclesiastics of a very high degree, and who should have known the proper address for a bishop, yet they use the expression "Exmo" that is "his excellency" which is entirely a civil dignity while a bishop's title is "Su Senoria" and in 1757 they had great care to use correct titles; yet these grand Inquisitors did not know the title of a bishop.

Of the Testaments.

These two instruments are written in the same peculiar bad Spanish of Ex. A and the photograph. The steryotyped beginning of them both are correct enough and must have been copied from some form book, or old wills, but the moment the testators come to the business on hand to inject into the body of the wills the pretended grant, the Caballero de los Colorados Grandee of Spain and his son Miguel de Peralta y Sanchez, suddenly lose all control of the Spanish language and begin to speak California cow-boy jargon.

The Caballero de los Colorados in Art. 5 of his will though he speaks throughout in the first person, when he mentions the grant of three hundred leagues says, speaking of this pretended grant "which was granted to Don Miguel de Peralta de la Cordoba y Caballero de los Colorados" as if this person was somebody else and not the testator himself. The will is signed by the testater; the notary says he did so, dated Jany. 3. 1783. Then follows a codicil in very bad Spanish, in which the name of the Caballero de los Colorados is said to be a copy, "es copia" but the notary and all the witnesses, the Bishop of Guatemala and the heir apparent, "the child" Miguel Peralta, join with genuine signatures; we see this plainly, because the claimant has furnished this office with a photographic copy of the notary's "minuta" or record.

The will appears to have been made in Mexico Jany. 3rd 1783 before a notary, Joseph Avalos. The codicil is made in Guadalajara, before a great number of witnesses including a bishop and a judge. The question arises, how did all these witnesses sign a codicil on the notarial records of a notary in the City of Mexico? and by what process did the notarial records of a Mexican notary get transported to Madrid?

And what force can a record that belongs in Mexico have when found in a foreign country? Even if Mexico now belonged to Spain this record would not probably be in Madrid, and could not be authenticated from there, so as to entitle it to any faith or credit.

We might attribute many of the features presented here, as the mistakes of an amanuensis, but the claimant has furnished us with photographic copies of the very record; and there appear the genuine signatures of seven witnesses, among them two lawyers, recited as being known for their truthfulness, a judge and the seal of his office, a bishop, who is of course infallible, and all these persons say they signed said document on Jany, 3rd, 1708? Just forty years before this pretended grant is dated. But there is nothing wonderful in the history of this alleged Peralta grant. To retrograde forty years is not as difficult a task as to make Ferdinand the VI and Charles III and all the grandees and dons of Spain of the last century, speak the cow-boy Spanish of California of our day. Napoleon said it and Reavis accomplished it, the word impossible is not in his dictionary.

There was no law in existence at the time, viz: 1783, that required a testament to be made before a notary, see Pandectos España Mexicano, Vol. 111 Partida 6, title 1, page 596. Nor had the said notary, by any law, the authority to enter into his records a copy or minutes of the said testament. Nor did such entry give it any force.

The original or true testament of which the Ex's in AAA & BBB are supposed to be copies, should be in the hands of the claimant, who should have received it from the adminis- trators of the ancestors, and on that will there should appear, under the certificate of the judge, where the Caballero de los Colorados died, that the witnesses were called, examined, and their testimony entered on the will itself, or attached to it, and so certified by the judge, the will should have been given to the "Albacea." A note of everything done, and the testimony of each witness signed by him, and all countersigned by the judge should and would have remained in the records of the court if they were genuine. Hence if the Caballero de los Colorados died at Guadalajara in 1788, the record of his will and the opening of it (what we call the probate of it) should be found in the archives of the judge of 1st instance in Guadalajara.

See Pandectas Esp. Mexicanos Vol. III, Partida 6, Title II, pg. 608. And this would have been the proper record to have been brought here to prove the existence of the will and the probation of it. We might just as well produce the notes from the minute book of a justice of the peace of our courts to prove the will of any person in Arizona.

We might just as well say here that the record, or notatorial archives of the notary "Joseph Avelas" located in the City of Mexico in 1783, should be to this day in the hands of his successor in office. For notaries in Spain and Mexico in the last and in the present century, even today, are officers of the state for certain purposes only, and beyond these purposes their acts are without authority, and their records are not private but public records, which are transferred to the successor of the incumbent after his death. See Pandectos Spano Mexicanos, Vol. I, page 414, Laws XXVI.

The notary in Spanish countries being the depositories of local transactions, their records are held as public for their localities, and when one of them dies, the judge immediately takes possession of his archives, and keeps them sealed till a successor is appointed, when he delivers them to him, setting a certain price or value which the new notary has to pay to the family of the deceased. See id—Law XXV.

I cannot see then how the records of a Mexican notary got transferred to the city of Madrid, in Spain.

Of the Testament of Miguel Peralta de la Cordoba y Sanchez. This testament purports to have been written by the said testator, and he calls himself a native of Campas (a little town in Sonora) and "residente en la actualidad," that is "now residing" in the city of Hermosillo, and this expression is characterized by bad Spanish.

The evident purpose of this will appears to have been to fix the family of the present alleged Baroness de los Colorados; as it describes in broken Spanish (spoken by a supposed native of Sonora, and son of a Grandee of Spain) the birth of Sophia and her marriage with Maso; then both conveniently die, leaving twins, a boy whose death is described in a jargon resembling Dutch, leaving Sophia Loreta Mecaela Maso y Peralta de la Cordoba, with a clear field to inherit alone the Baronial estate of Peralta. Then it goes on, and undertakes by his own declarations to prove the great Peralta grant, by copying the whole of Ex. A only that there are some few changes made in order to make it better as herein above noted. This will is made out at Hermosillo, but like everything else in this pretended Peralta grant, a notary of San Francisco is made to officiate as the attesting officer, without witnesses, dated Jan. 2nd, 1863.

This alleged Peralta grant is full of surprises. An ordinary mortal would have had his will authenticated by residents of the place where he is. Mr. Peralta gets a notary of San Francisco to do it.

Again, this alleged Peralta, appears at the "Villa de Madrid," before another notary—Bernardo Diaz de Antonana (as we might say the village of New York) and makes a codicil, marked as Article 11th, and in worse Spanish than any prior attempt, reiterating the fact that the present claimant provides that the Countess Sophia, etc., etc., is to take possession of the Peralta property.

The notary here says that the original will and papers and maps were sent to the administrator appointed, to-wit, to Antonio Pablo Peralta, of San Bernardino, California, and that he, the said notary, kept copies of all of said papers.

This will, as it comes before this office as to the notarial record, etc., etc., is subject to the same remarks herein above made as to that of the Caballero de los Colorados himself.

However this third paper brings out some new features of importance. In the prior will, this same testator Miguel Peralta de la Cordoba, signs the codicil with his own hand, though he is called "nino," child. That was in 1788. Now he makes his will and the notary declares that the old gentleman, in April 11th of 1865, was 84 years of age. By an easy calculation this testator appears to have been only five years old in 1788, when his signature indicates an old practiced hand. For we have his photographic copy as furnished by claimant on file in this office.

It appears then that the original will is somewhere on this continent, and it should be produced.

Of the testimony presented by the photograph of two pages of a book of records of the Mission of San Javier del Bac.

These photos show on their face that they are forgeries, interpolated in said book by interested parties:

1st. Because the handwriting is entirely different and made in different ink and with a steel pen.

2nd. Because the said inscription begins with the Jesuit monogram I H J which to use was tantamont to being thrown into prison in 1788, because Father Pauer (Paver) was in 1767 expelled from Spanish-America and Spain to Italy, and it would have been death for him to be at San Javier del Bac in 1788. See Bancroft's History of Mexico Northern States Vol. XV; pages 549–580. The Jesuits left Sonora in the beginning of 1768, see page 578.

3rd. The testimony of Thomas H. McMullen shows that he has seen and examined the original book of parts of which these photographs were made, and that the page or sheet upon which the entry is made, that the claimant relies upon, has been interpolated since the book was bound, that the paper is entirely different from that made use of in the remainder of the book.

This alleged Peralta grant was not made or executed in the forms and in the manner required by the customs and laws of the times 1748 to 1776.

Though the kings of Spain were absolute monarchs at that time, yet in order to transact the business of so vast an empire they themselves established certain rules and regulations, certain channels and ministers to carry out their will and govern their dominions.

For an instance, any order the king made, signed by his name "Yo el Rey" had the force of law all over the Spanish empire yet such a document in Spain would have had no force if it was not countersigned by his prime minister.

In the government of his American possessions the king of Spain made the Laws 1st, 2nd and 3rd Title I, Book 2nd "de la Recompilacion de Indias" and law 40 Title I, Book 20 of the "Nueva Recompilacion" which laws provide that no decree, law, order or cedula, made by the king should have any force or effect in the American Colonies belonging to Spain, unless such law, decree, order or cedula was adopted by the "Consejo de Indias" and published by that body where it was intended to take effect.

See also Bancroft's History of Mexico, Vol. XI. page 519.

See also Hall's Mexican Law, page 13. Here at the end of a cedula of the king it has these words "Dated in Pardo the 1st of Nov. 1591. I, the King. By order of the king our lord Juan de Harrar. By decree of the 12th of March 1593, it was ordered that the foregoing royal cedula should be obeyed and published. And Bancroft, in the page above quoted says: "Its jurisdiction (the council of the Indies) extended to every department, civil, military, ecclesiastic and commercial, even the Pope having here to submit for approval his bulls and briefs concerning the Indies."

But where is this pretended cedula of the alleged Peralta referred for consideration and approval? To the Chamber of the Holy Tribunal of the Inquisition of the City of Mexico! It is assumed that Peralta was so great a man and his privileges were so great that the king resolved to break through the "Customs of the Crown" and all existing laws, pass over the heads of his council of the Indies, which superintended even the commands of the Popes, and ordered the viceroy to grant the land; that in spite of the laws above quoted, by which the king's command of their viceroys and governors of all his dominions in America, that under no circumstances even his own orders should be respected or obeyed unless the same had received the sanction of the "Consejo de Indias" in the face of all these laws and customs, the viceroy did give effect to the cedula in favor of Peralta. And yet the name of this pretended great man is not found in the history of Spain or Mexico. Then again this cedula it is claimed, was first approved by the Council of the Inquisition, who never did have the power to receive, consider or approve cedulas of the king.

Then again it is claimed that this same council of the Holy Inquisition took upon itself the task of finding the location of the pretended grant and that upon its recommendation the viceroy ordered Peralta *himself* with the help of a Jesuit priest to go and locate and survey the said grant to suit his own exclusive will and fancy.

And where did Peralta locate his three hundred leagues? Why, it is claimed that he went to Sonora, to the Prineria Alta, outside of the jurisdiction of the viceroy of New Spain, and located them. And that the viceroy granted them to him.

And it is further claimed that all this chain of blunders is finally approved by Charles III in 1776 and referred for record to the Holy Tribunal of the Inquisition of Mexico.

Having exposed the first blunder in this pretended grant namely: that it did not pass before the "Consejo de Indias" we come to the second that it was submitted to the Inquisition.

We may read all the history of Spanish America and all the laws contained in the recompilations of Spain and of the Indies, and we have yet to see where this tribunal, whose institution was established to burn heretics and Turks, was empowered to measure, locate or deliver possession of land. It is incumbent on the claimant to prove the law under which the proceedings in his pretended grant were executed; this he has totally failed to do. See Hall's Mx law, Chap. II. In this chapter is a compilation of the land laws of Spain, which was entirely under the control of the civil branch of the Government, and nowhere do we see that the inquisition or any priest had the granting or surveying of lands except in the following cases. The only instance where we find the priests acting as grantors of lands is in the early missionary period of Lower California and Pimeria of Sonora, but that was when the Jesuits were empowered to manage both the civil and the ecclesiastical affairs, and then, their power was limited to granting lots and small farms near the Pueblos and Missions. But this priestly rule did not last long, and we see that in 1693 a Governor was appointed in Sonora. See Bancroft's, XV page 258; and that in 1734 Sonora and Sinaloa were raised to the dignity of an independent province, subject only to the viceroy of Mexico as subordinates in military matters, yet even in military matters the viceroy did not have an independent power in Sonora, and what power he did exercise was not independent of the Governor of Sonora, but through him. See Bancroft's XV, page 520. From 1734 down to and since 1776, the period covered by the proceedings here mentioned, this state of things continued. In certain civil proceedings and for all matters concerning lands, Sonora belonged to the dominion of the Audiencia of Guadalajara that is Nueva Galicia.

We find in Hall's Mx laws, page 5, Sec. 12, that under the land laws of 1754, which cover the period here in question, Sonora was in land matters under the jurisdiction of the Audiencia of Guadalajara, which had the disposal of lands therein. The law itself of 1754, is fully set forth in Hall's Mx. laws, page 26.

This pretended Peralta grant was petitioned for in 1748,

SURVEYOR GENERAL'S REPORT.   105

directly to the King and in this respect only might the proceeding have been regular, because at that period the law so provided. See Hall's Mexican law, page 14, Sec. 27.

But it is not pretended that anything was done with the Peralta claim till the report of the inquisitors in October 10th, 1757, just four years after the new law had come into effect, and after the power to grant lands was delegated by the King to the Audiencias of Mexico for the Southern provinces, and to that of Gualalajara for the northern provinces of North America. See Hall's Mexican laws, page 17. et seq.

Anyway, if Peralta claims his grant was under the law of 1735, that law only goes as far as to reserve to the King, the right to receive petitions for lands and confirm them after they have been located, surveyed and determined, leaving all those formalities to be settled under the laws in book 4, title 12. In these laws, it is expressly said that all the intermediate steps between the petition and the approval of the Kings, shall be made by the viceroy, Governor or other civil officer having jurisdiction of the locality.

But the law of 1754 does not leave any room to doubt that all proceedings or incomplete grants after that date had to be governed by the new law, and that the grants were required to be made by the Audiencias. Hall's Mx. law, page 31-32, Sec. 66.

This law prescribes who shall make the surveys and who shall make the grant; what proceedings must be followed, all in a minute and detailed manner.

According to the laws both of 1735 and 1754 the proceedings in this case should be as follows, viz: The cedula of the King should:

1st. Have been sanctioned by the "Concijo de Indias."

2nd. It should have been remitted to the viceroy, who should have endorsed it, and then,

3rd. Remitted it to the Captain General, or Governor of Sonora or Sinaloa, the land being located in his jurisdiction.

4th. The Governor of Sonora should have endorsed it, and added an order to the head of the civil and military authority at Tubac, which was the northernmost military post and presidio under direct civil Spanish rule at the time. (See Bancroft XV, page 559.) To go to the place chosen by the claimant, and start the proceedings by making publication, calling all neighbors and former grantees to appear and present objections if they had any.

5th. The report in full of all the proceedings, testimony, survey certified to, returned to the Governor.

6th. The Governor endorsing the proceedings, sends them to the Audiencia of Guadalajara who issues its grant.

7th. These Procotols, which by this time in the Peralto claim should have amounted to a small volume of fifty closely written pages is kept by the Audiencia, and a copy of it, with the original deed of grant attached on the last page of the expedients should have been given to Peralta. (Hall's Mx. law, page 71, Sec. 172-1773.)

As this pretended Peralta grant if ever made, was issued under two laws; initiated under law of 1735 and finished under law of 1754 it should be found in the records.

1st. Of Madrid.

2nd. Of a Viceroy of Mexico.

3rd. In records of the Audencia of Guadalajara. (See Hall's Mx. law, page 73, Sec. 174-177-1778.

When in fact not one of those requisite steps appear to have been taken and no evidence is found in either of the places where it would be if the grant had actually been made.

Many grants made from 1648 to 1800 now found in the archives of Sonora have been examined and in none of them are found the bad Spanish used in this pretended cedula.

The golden age of the Castilian language was the sixteenth century when Calderon, De la Vega, Cervantes and many others wrote, and their works then crystallized the language, and made it what it is now; and those who pretend to speak Castilian well take the pattern from those authors.

This pretended cedula has more faults in it than it has words. One word often has two and three mistakes of orthography and grammar.

The whole thing is a bold attempt of some person ignorant

of Spanish history, law or language. Even the stereotyped form employed in the cedula of the Kings of Spain is wanting. In this pretended cedula of Ferdinand VI or that of Carlos III, the King commences his decree in the same manner as any other mortal; in the one it commences:

"El Rey virrey Governador y Capitan General," and the other, that of Carlos III is characterized by the same simplicity; whereas the forms made use of by Carlos III in all his cedulas occupied many lines in a preliminary recital of his titles. The following is the form usually employed by Carlos III as appears by an examination of his published cedulas known to be genuine, viz:

"Don Carlos, Por la Gracia De Dios Rey de Castilla, de Leon, de Aragon, de las dos Sicilias, de Jerusalen, de Navarra, de Granada, de Toledo, de Valencia, de Galicia, de Mallorca, de Sevilla, de Cerdeña, de Cordova, de Corcega, de Murcia, de Jaen, de los Algarves, de Algecira, de Gibraltar, de las Islas de Canaria, de las Indias Orientales, y Occidentales Islas y Tierra-Firme del Mar Oceano, Archiduque de Austria, Duque de Borgona, de Bravante, y Milan, Conde de Abspurg, Flandes, Tirol, Barcelona, Senor de Vizcaya, y de Molina, etc., etc." Even these common and usual recitals in the cedulas of the kings of Spain are utterly ignored; and the pretended cedula recommending the grant to be made by the Viceroy of New Spain follow the simple form now in use by the presidents of the several republics in the world; which corroborates the correctness of the view herein expressed that these documents were prepared by persons who never lived under a monarchical government, but whose education, inspiration and surroundings were those found only among the people who reside on the Pacific Coast of the United States of America.

I therefore respectfully submit that this claim is entirely unsupported by any evidence; and that it should be given no recognition by the government of the United States under the treaty between the Republic of Mexico and the United States.

Respectfully submitted,
CLARK CHURCHILL,
Counsel for settlers upon lands covered by the pretended grant.

www.ingramcontent.com/pod-product-compliance
Lightning Source LLC
Chambersburg PA
CBHW022146160426
43197CB00009B/1446